Basic Training
for the Prophetic Ministry

Basic Training
for the Prophetic Ministry

Kris Vallotton

Destiny Image. Publishers, Inc.

P.O. Box 310

Shippensburg, PA 17257-0310

"Speaking to the Purposes of God for this Generation
and for the Generations to Come."

For Worldwide Distribution, Printed in the U.S.A.

ISBN 10: 0-7684-2444-5

ISBN 13: 978-0-7684-2444-7

Previously published as *A Call to War*.

This book and all other Destiny Image, Revival Press, MercyPlace, Fresh Bread, Destiny Image Fiction, and Treasure House books are available at Christian bookstores and distributors worldwide.

For a U.S. bookstore nearest you, call
1-800-722-6774.

For more information on foreign distributors, call
717-532-3040.

Or reach us on the Internet:
www.destinyimage.com

6 7 8 9 10 11 12 13 / 14 13 12 11 10

Contents

Foreword

A new generation of soaring prophetic eagles is now here among us. These risk-taking believers in the Lord Jesus Christ are not somewhere "out there" in the far distant future—they are with us now.

Kris Vallotton and his crew at Bethel Church's School of the Supernatural in Redding, California, seem to be leading the way! They have the highest level of impartation of any school of the supernatural that I know of anywhere today. Yes, that's right!

This generation of radical warriors is cut from a cloth different from my generation. We came from religion and learned the supernatural. But this generation is birthed in the supernatural and is soaring high in the things of God at an early age.

Wow—so where does that leave those in my generation? Are we left to be the bystanders just applauding the exploits of the new Joshua's and Caleb's? Absolutely not! There are new vistas for us each. In fact, I tell some of my students, "You are going to have to run fast to catch me 'cause I'm about to catch my second (or third) wind and I will outrun you all!" I think you get my drift.

Let me drive home my point by telling you one of my wife's many significant dreams. There was a line of men and women all standing neatly in a row—my wife, Michal Ann, was positioned there among them. An invitation was given by the Holy Spirit for fathers and mothers in the prophetic to step forward. In the dream, all of the others took a step backward so it appeared as though Michal Ann had just volunteered. Then a strong gust of wind hit her from behind and flung her even farther forward.

She was awakened out of the dream knowing somehow that she had just been chosen, or had volunteered with help, to be a mother of the prophetic in her generation. It has been amazing to watch what the Lord has done with this once withdrawn dear lady who has been thrust to the front of God's prophetic compassion army. If it could happen to Michal Ann and James W. Goll—it can happen to anyone! Remember—He is not a respecter of persons. He is looking for fresh volunteers at all times. There is room in His army for you!

That is what the manual you hold in your hands is about—Basic Training for the Prophetic Ministry. It is one of God's tools for this time and day, written from the trenches of great experience. My friend, Kris Vallotton, is one of the fathers in the making. Yes, there are many fathers and mothers who are volunteering to raise up the voice of the Lord.

Want to join them? Then tear apart this book. Lean in and learn all you can. Then take your hands out of your pockets, get your feet outside of the four walls of your church and home, open wide your mouth, and let the Holy Spirit fill it. Do something for Jesus' sake!

This manual is a call for passionate, consecrated warriors to arise. Therefore, it is with deep admiration and joy that I have the privilege of commending this training guide to you. Join Kris and I and a new breed generation who are learning to fly high in the things of the Holy Spirit and take others with them. Volunteer freely in the day of His power and join His call to war!

—Dr. James W. Goll

Cofounder of Encounters Network
Author of *The Seer, Dream Language,*
The Coming Prophetic Revolution, and many others.
www.jamesgoll.com

Preface

This book was not written to be the final word on prophetic ministry. The goal was to help develop and facilitate prophetic communities. In addition to teaching how to minister prophetically, I also share a prospective that promotes a healthy community of believers. Therefore, I have intentionally emphasized instruction, which will assist leaders in shepherding the prophetic people of their communities.

With this in mind, there are thought-provoking questions and a Life Application section at the end of each chapter. The answers to the Questions to Ponder are found within the chapters. The Group Discussions Questions are not directly answered in the chapters, but are to provoke thought and stimulate discussion. We often learn more through our own discovery than we do from someone else's teaching. These questions should help facilitate the discovery process.

The purpose of the Life Application section is to help you get past the obstacles that keep you from moving ahead in the prophetic ministry. There are also ideas about how to practically apply what you are learning.

My earnest prayer is that every Christian who reads this book will be drawn closer to God, and will join us in destroying the works of the devil.

Let the journey begin!

"It is you who are the sons of the prophets...."
(Acts 3:25)

"...he who believes in Me, the works that I do, he will do also; and greater works than these he will do; because I go to the Father"
(John 14:12)

Introduction

In the days of the prophet Elijah, there arose a company of men who were called the "sons of the prophets." These men traveled throughout the world ravaging the powers of darkness, wreaking havoc on evil kingdoms. They had no tolerance for the destructive behavior of wicked kings but rather turned many to righteousness. They raised the dead, healed the sick, parted rivers, destroyed false prophets, and saw revival spread throughout their land. They were feared by many and respected by all. They walked in great purity; and God was their friend.

Today, all around us, wickedness continues to grow, taking root in the lives of those we love and eroding the very foundation of our country. Satanism is spreading like wildfire. Psychics laugh in the face of the church as they demonstrate the power of the dark side. Divorce is destroying our families and violence is corrupting our children. Sickness and diseases take the lives of so many. Yet the words of our Lord Jesus echo through the halls of history, "...*he who believes in Me, the works that I do, he will do also; and greater works than these he will do; because I go to the Father*" (John 14:12).

In Acts 3:25, Peter says, "*It is you who are the sons of the prophets....*" It is time for the Body of Christ to rise up and receive our inheritance! We must rid ourselves of complacency and restore the ancient boundaries of holiness and demonstrations of great power. We cannot be satisfied with illustrative sermons, great music, and friendly services. We have been called to see the powers of darkness destroyed and our ruined cities restored.

In the days of Moses, God demonstrated His power to Pharaoh, but Pharaoh counter-attacked by having his sorcerers duplicate the miracles of God. Then the God of Heaven, who has all power, performed *extraordinary miracles* so that even the sorcerers said, "*This must be God. We cannot perform these miracles.*" Finally Pharaoh was overcome by God's power and let His people go. (See Exodus 7-12.)

I believe that the Pharaoh of this age is about to let go of our cities as God demonstrates His raw power through His Church. We are in the midst of the greatest revival in human history. Yet there remains a distance between what *should be* and what *will be*.

That distance is *you*! What will you be?

You are the bridge between history and *His story*.

You are the sons of the prophets!

The sick, the demonized, the poor, the blind, the lame, and the lost are waiting to see what you have learned.

Don't disappoint them!

The Purpose of Prophetic Ministry

This chapter explores the impact that prophecy has on people and the core values that should motivate prophetic ministry.

Prophetic Ministry—Looking for Treasure

The price that Jesus paid on the Cross determined the value of the people He purchased. God saw something good in us even when we were sinners. It doesn't take a prophetic gift to see the sin in sinners or the junk in the lives of Christians. It does require the eyes of God, though, to see broken people like Simon (Simon means "broken reed") and in the midst of their brokenness, call them Peter (Peter means "rock"). True prophetic ministry is looking for gold in the midst of the dirt in people's lives.

Finding Treasure in the Life of Sinners

Paul tells us in First Corinthians that prophecy reveals the secrets of unbeliever's hearts.

But if all prophesy, and an unbeliever or an ungifted man enters, he is convicted by all, he is called to account by all; the secrets of his heart are disclosed; and so he will fall on his face and worship God, declaring that God is certainly among you. (1 Corinthians 14: 24-25)

Notice in the passage that the person who receives the prophetic word doesn't repent but rather "*will fall on his face and worship God.*" Most people know what is wrong with them but they are unaware of the greatness that God has placed in their lives. Remember that Jesus didn't just die for our sins but He offered up His life because we "*fell short of the glory of God*" (see Rom. 3:23). Prophecy brings people into a revelation of the glory that God has assigned to them. This exposure brings conviction in their lives that they are living below the glorious standard that God has set for them.

> ## Prophecy reveals the secrets in unbeliever's hearts.

Prophetic Ministry Can Change People's Hearts

In the ninth chapter of First Samuel there is a stirring story of prophetic ministry redirecting someone's heart.

Saul has been sent by his father to find their lost donkeys. After an unsuccessful venture, they decide to go to the nearest city to ask direction from a certain prophet. Meanwhile, God tells Samuel that Saul is coming to him to find his donkeys, and amazingly, he is to anoint him king of Israel. When Saul finally encounters Samuel, the prophet informs him that his donkeys are already found. Then he stuns Saul by asking him to stay until the next day in order to tell him all that is in his mind because he is the man in whom all the desires of Israel lie. Saul is shocked and says to Samuel, "*Am I not a Benjamite, of the smallest of the tribes of Israel, and my family the least of all the families of the tribe of Benjamin? Why then do you speak to me in this way?*" (1 Sam. 9:21).

Low self-esteem has caused many people to lose sight of the greatness that God has placed in them. Notice that Samuel says he is going to tell him what is *already* in his mind (literally *heart*). The story goes on to describe how Samuel anoints Saul king and tells him that he is going to encounter a group of prophets coming down from the hills. When he joins them, he will be changed into another man. By the time Saul turned to leave, he was changed into another man. He was transformed back into the man that he was *designed to be from the beginning*. The real man who was hidden under low self-esteem and sin was revealed and restored. This is the heart of true prophetic ministry!

Samuel answered Saul and said, "I am the seer. Go up before me to the high place, for you shall eat with me today; and in the morning I will let you go, and will tell you all that is on your mind. As for your donkeys which were lost three days ago, do not set your mind on them, for they have been found And for whom is all that is desirable in Israel? Is it not for you and for all your father's household?" Saul replied, "Am I not a Benjamite, of the smallest of the tribes of Israel, and my family the least of all the families of the tribe of Benjamin? Why then do you speak to me in this way?" Then Samuel took Saul and his servant and brought them into the

hall and gave them a place at the head of those who were invited, who were about thirty men (1 Samuel 9:19-22).

Afterward you will come to the hill of God where the Philistine garrison is; and it shall be as soon as you have come there to the city, that you will meet a group of prophets coming down from the high place with harp, tambourine, flute, and a lyre before them, and they will be prophesying. Then the Spirit of the Lord will come upon you mightily, and you shall prophesy with them and be changed into another man (1 Samuel 10:5-6).

Does Greatness Promote Pride?

Some believe that calling out greatness in people promotes pride. True humility is not thinking *less of yourself* but thinking of yourself *less*. The truth of God's grace humbles a man without degrading him and exalts a man without inflating him.

> *Some time ago I was teaching on the purposes of prophetic ministry. Beginning with a few opening comments, I said: "Prophecy calls out the greatness in people."*
>
> *Just then a pastor walked through the back door and said, "I have a question."*
>
> *"What is it?"*
>
> *"I believe that God is great," he said.*
>
> *"Yes. Did I say something that made you feel that God wasn't great?"*
>
> *"You said we are to call out the greatness in people. I believe that you are creating pride in people by doing that," he said.*
>
> *I fired back, "I believe that for years the church has emasculated and castrated people in the name of humility." I pointed to a beautiful painting on the wall and said, "Let's pretend you painted that picture."*
>
> *"OK," he said, looking confused.*
>
> *"That's a stupid looking painting! Look at those ugly colors!" I yelled. "Now," I asked him, "Did demeaning the painting glorify the artist?"*
>
> *"No" he said.*

> *"Isn't it true that the beauty of the painting actually brings honor to the artist?"*
>
> *"Yes, that's true," he said.*
>
> *"You didn't paint yourself—God painted you," I told him. "Not only that, but Jesus is the one who sat in the chair and modeled for the portrait. We are created in His image and in His likeness. Every time we demean ourselves we are talking badly about the Artist and the Model. The truth is that the beauty of creation actually gives glory to the Creator."*

True Humility Expressed

There is an interesting story in Daniel chapter 4. Nebuchadnezzar has a dream about a large, beautiful tree being cut down by an angel. Daniel interprets the dream to mean that "Nebs" is about to lose his mind for seven years because of his arrogance and pride. He will become like an animal until he recognizes that God is the ruler of the world. Twelve months later, the king is on the roof of his castle telling himself how awesome he is for having built Babylon with his own strength and power.

Just then he goes insane. He becomes like an animal, living in the fields eating grass. After seven years, his sanity returns. Look at the first words Nebuchadnezzar says when he could finally speak instead of mumble:

At that time my reason returned to me and my majesty and splendor were restored to me for the glory of my kingdom, and my counselors and my nobles began seeking me out; so I was reestablished in my sovereignty, and surpassing greatness was added to me. Now I, Nebuchadnezzar, praise, exalt and honor the King of Heaven, for all His works are true and His ways just, and He is able to humble those who walk in pride (Daniel 4:36-37).

Nebuchadnezzar is saying, "I am humbly awesome!" Humility is not demeaning yourself, it is exalting our God!

Questions to Ponder

1. What is the main purpose for prophetic ministry?

looking for the gold in the midst of the dirt in people's lives

2. What did we fall short of when we were sinners?

glory of God

3. What are the secrets of people's hearts?

4. What is true humility?

Exalting God

5. Who were you modeled after when you were created?

Jesus

Questions for Group Discussion

1. How can I be involved with evil people and still call out the greatness in them?

2. Is there a time when it is wrong to show people the glory that God has hidden in them?

Life Application

Think of one person in your life with whom you have the most problems. Spend some time praying for that person. Ask the Holy Spirit to reveal to you one aspect of the glory of God that is assigned to that person. Now, go tell that person what you see and observe how this affects your relationship.

"It is you who are the sons of the prophets...."
(Acts 3:25)

"...he who believes in Me, the works that I do, he will do also; and greater works than these he will do; because I go to the Father"
(John 14:12)

BASIC TRAINING BASIC

Chapter 2

Prophets and Prophecy

Have you ever wondered what the difference is between the Gift of Prophecy and the Office of Prophet? In this chapter the many mysteries that have baffled the church for generations are unraveled.

The Gift of Prophecy

The gift of prophecy is one of the nine gifts of the Holy Spirit.

Now there are varieties of gifts, but the same Spirit. And there are varieties of ministries, and the same Lord. There are varieties of effects, but the same God who works all things in all persons. But to each one is given the manifestation of the Spirit for the common good. For to one is given the word of wisdom through the Spirit, and to another the word of knowledge according to the same Spirit; to another faith by the same Spirit, and to another gifts of healing by the one Spirit, and to another the effecting of miracles, and to another prophecy, and to another the distinguishing of spirits, to another various kinds of tongues, and to another the interpretation of tongues. But one and the same Spirit works all these things, distributing to each one individually just as He wills (1 Corinthians 12:4-11).

We are to earnestly desire spiritual gifts. Earnestly desire means to "lust after"—God wants us to pursue His gifts! He desires to give us His gifts more than we could ever want them.

*Pursue love, yet **desire earnestly** spiritual gifts, but especially that you may prophesy. For one who speaks in a tongue does not speak to men but to God; for no one understands, but in his spirit he speaks mysteries. But one who prophesies speaks to men for edification and exhortation and consolation (1 Corinthians 14:1-3, emphasis added).*

Prophecy Is a *Gift*—Not an *Award*

We didn't earn it! We received it by asking. This means that even very gifted people are not necessarily mature Christians. They may not even have good character. Therefore, the gifts of the Spirit do not validate our walk with God. It is the fruit of the Spirit that is developed as a person matures in Christ. The Greek word for *gift* is "charisma," which means, "favor that one receives without any merit of his own." The *fruit* of the Spirit is the evidence of maturity in our lives. These fruits grow in our lives as we allow the Holy Spirit to work *in* us and not just *through* us.

But the fruit of the Spirit is love, joy, peace, patience, kindness, goodness, faithfulness, gentleness, self-control; against such things there is no law (Galatians 5:22-23).

The gift of prophecy is for the purpose of edification, exhortation, and consolation. *Edification* means "to build up." *Exhortation* means, "to call near." *Consolation* means "to cheer up."

To Encourage the Church

The primary purpose of the gift of prophecy is not to *direct or correct* the Body of Christ, but rather to **encourage** *the church*. We should never allow people who are ministering in the gift of prophecy to speak negatively into the lives of others. The *goal* of the gift of prophecy is to **bring out the best in people!** We are to mine the gold that is within the dirt and find hidden treasures in people's lives. If we see negative things in someone's life we are ministering to, we are to ask the Holy Spirit to give us the answer to the problem we discern. Then we *prophesy the answer—not the problem.* That way, the person we are prophesying to will receive grace to solve their problem.

For example, if we are ministering to someone and discern that they are struggling with pornography, the Holy Spirit will often give us a prophetic word for them such as: "*God is calling you to a new level of purity and holiness.*" In this way, we have prophesied the answer without speaking about the *problem* and have released grace to break the bondage of pornography.

Prophecy encourages the Church.

Anyone who is saved and receives the baptism of the Holy Spirit can minister in the gifts of the Spirit.

For you can all prophesy one by one, so that all may learn and all may be exhorted (1 Corinthians 14:31).

"And it shall be in the last days," God says, "That I will pour forth of My Spirit on all mankind; and your sons and your daughters shall prophesy, and your young men shall see visions, and your old men shall dream dreams; even on My bond-slaves, both men and women, I will in those days pour forth of My Spirit and they shall prophesy" (Acts 2:17-18).

Prophets

Christ gave the prophets to the church as a gift. The main function of a prophet is to equip the saints to do the work of service. The prophet equips the church with *eyes to see* and *ears to hear*. The grace that prophets carry can literally cause people to be able to hear the voice of the Spirit. Prophets have the authority to correct and direct because they are a part of the government of God.

The Calling of a Prophet or Prophetess

The office of the prophet is a life calling. Most prophets are called at birth or when they are born again. I do not believe that this is something you ask for or seek to become. It is the *Lord's* choosing. However, if you are called, you still have the responsibility to develop your gift. I remember hearing Graham Cooke say many years ago during a conference: "It takes fourteen years for a person to develop into a prophet after being called."

But to each one of us grace was given according to the measure of Christ's gift. Therefore it says, "When He ascended on high, He led captive a host of captives, and

He gave gifts to men." (Now this expression, "He ascended," what does it mean except that He also had descended into the lower parts of the earth? He who descended is Himself also He who ascended far above all the heavens, so that He might fill all things.) And He gave some as apostles, and some as prophets, and some as evangelists, and some as pastors and teachers, for the equipping of the saints for the work of service, to the building up of the body of Christ; until we all attain to the unity of the faith, and of the knowledge of the Son of God, to a mature man, to the measure of the stature which belongs to the fullness of Christ (Ephesians 4:7-13).

In order for us to receive the grace that allows us to see and hear (which is the *prophet's reward*), we must *receive the prophet in the name of a prophet.*

*He who receives a prophet in the name of a prophet shall receive a **prophet's reward**; and he who receives a righteous man in the name of a righteous man shall receive a righteous man's reward* (Matthew 10:41, emphasis added).

Each of us receives from people based on the role that we understand them to play in our lives. For example, someone seeking counsel from a prophet must realize that, unlike a pastor (whose best counsel comes after much listening), a prophet will often give his or her best insight with little or no prior information. A person trying to receive this type of counsel without understanding the gift and role of the prophet may think to themselves, "How can you give me counsel when you don't even understand my situation?" Therefore, it is important for us to understand the various roles that the members of the Body of Christ play in our lives.

The Fivefold Ministry

The following is a very brief overview of the governmental offices in the church. Included is a short description of their roles in the Body of Christ, giving understanding and assistance in receiving their ministry into our lives.

Apostles *govern.* Apostles are similar to the general contractor who oversees the project and sees the overall picture.

Prophets *guide.* Prophets are the architects who assist the general contractor to know what the project should look like.

Evangelists *gather.* Evangelists' concern is for the lost.

Pastors *guard*. A pastor's heart is for the saved.

Teachers *ground*. A teacher's primary role is to help the flock understand the Word of God.

Paul did *not* say, "*I* have the mind of Christ." He said, "*We* have the mind of Christ." (See 1 Corinthians 2:16.) We gain the balance we need and God's perspective on situations when we learn to value the members of the Body who think differently than we do!

The Difference Between Prophets and Prophecy

To be a prophet is a *calling*.

To minister in prophecy is a *gift*.

When a person ministers in the gift of prophecy, the *gift* is the *ability to prophesy*. The words themselves are the gift. When a person is a prophet, *they themselves* are the gift. The Book of Ephesians says, Christ gave gifts to men. The gifts that Christ gave to men are *other men*. A prophet is a gift to the church.

There are actually three components to any mature ministry. These components include calling, gifting, and anointing—all important elements of fruitful ministry.

Calling gives identity. "*Paul, called as an apostle of Jesus Christ by the will of God*" (1 Cor. 1:1).

Gifting gives ability. "*As each one has received a special gift, employ it in serving one another as good stewards of the manifold grace of God*" (1 Pet. 4:10).

Anointing gives purpose. "*The Spirit of the Lord God is upon me, because the Lord has anointed me to bring good news to the afflicted; He has sent me to bind up the brokenhearted, to proclaim liberty to captives and freedom to prisoners*" (Isa. 61:1).

The gifts and callings of God are irrevocable but the anointing of the Lord ebbs and flows according to the relationship we have with the Holy Spirit.

Therefore, we must realize that the calling on our life describes *who* we are. The anointing of God provides us with our *purpose* in life. The gifts that God has given to us become the abilities in which we accomplish His purposes.

The gifts and the calling of God are irrevocable (Romans 11:29).

Prophecy Defined

Prophecy in the purist sense is *foretelling* and *forthtelling*.

Foretelling—to *know* the future.

The following is an example of foretelling. Agabus speaks prophetically about a famine that will take place all over the world. It happens a few years later.

> *One of them named Agabus stood up and began to indicate by the Spirit that there would certainly be a great famine all over the world. And this took place in the reign of Claudius* (Acts 11:28).

Forthtelling—to *cause* the future.

A great example of forthtelling is in the following passages in Ezekiel. God instructs the prophet Ezekiel to prophesy to dead bones and they became a mighty army. Ezekiel just didn't *tell* the future he *caused* the future!

> *The hand of the Lord was upon me, and He brought me out by the Spirit of the Lord and set me down in the middle of the valley; and it was full of bones. He caused me to pass among them round about, and behold, there were very many on the surface of the valley; and lo, they were very dry.*
>
> *He said to me, "Son of man, can these bones live?" And I answered, "O Lord God, You know." Again He said to me, "Prophesy over these bones and say to them, 'O dry bones, hear the word of the Lord.' Thus says the Lord God to these bones, 'Behold, I will cause breath to enter you that you may come to life. I will put sinews on you, make flesh grow back on you, cover you with skin and put breath in you that you may come alive; and you will know that I am the Lord.'"*
>
> *So I prophesied as I was commanded; and as I prophesied, there was a noise, and behold, a rattling; and the bones came together, bone to its bone. And I looked, and behold, sinews were on them, and flesh grew and skin covered them; but there was no breath in them. Then He said to me, "Prophesy to the breath, prophesy, son of man, and say to the breath, 'Thus says the Lord God, "Come from the four winds, O breath, and breathe on these slain, that they come to life."'"*

So I prophesied as He commanded me, and the breath came into them, and they came to life and stood on their feet, an exceedingly great army (Ezekiel 37:1-10).

Word of Knowledge

People often confuse the word of knowledge with the gift of prophecy. The word of knowledge describes something that took place in the past, a current circumstance, or a fact about someone's life. Sometimes when we prophesy, someone can mistakenly think that the prophecy wasn't accurate because it is not something that is currently happening, or has ever happened in that person's life. Pure prophecy is about the *future*. If the prophetic word lacks an element of something that has already taken place, this simply means that the word of knowledge was not part of the delivery. A word of knowledge is simply knowing a *fact*, revealed by the Holy Spirit, of which we had no prior knowledge.

Levels of Prophecy

There are generally four levels of prophecy.

Level 1—Prophetic Culture

A prophetic culture takes place when a prophet or high level prophetic anointing is present in a geographic location—in this atmosphere, even non-prophetic people can prophesy, although they may never prophesy again. This is demonstrated in the life of King Saul. When he was pursuing David in the wilderness, he encountered a group of prophets who were prophesying in the desert. Suddenly, the Spirit of prophecy fell upon Saul and he prophesied along with the prophets even though he was wicked! The people asked, *"Is Saul among the prophets?"* (1 Sam. 19:23-24), People ministering on this level are actually operating out of someone else's anointing. You might say they are borrowing from someone else. In a prophetic atmosphere, even a *donkey* can speak for God!

Level 2—The Gift of Prophecy

This second level of prophecy has been discussed earlier in this chapter. It is simply the Holy Spirit's gifts working in and through a person. Most of the information in this book is dedicated to this level of prophecy.

Level 3—Prophetic People

These people are not prophets because that is not the call on their lives; but they operate in the Holy Spirit's gift at a high level. They also have a proven prophetic ministry and they have a strong relationship with the church leadership. Therefore, they are often allowed to direct and perhaps even correct people within their local congregation. This type of trusted relationship can take years to develop.

Level 4—Prophets and Prophetesses

This is the highest level of prophetic ministry, which was mentioned previously.

The Three Parts of Prophecy

Revelation: The person who gives the prophetic word is responsible for the revelation of the word. It may come as a dream, a vision, or any of the ways that are explained in the next chapter.

Interpretation: What does the revelation mean? Prophetic people need to realize that just because they had the revelation does not mean that they have the interpretation. We often get into trouble when we try to interpret a vision or some other form of God's voice.

Application: What should we do with the word once we know what it means? Our pastor or overseer should always be involved when the prophetic word includes direction. They should help the recipient of the word devise a plan to actually apply it to their life and walk it out.

The easiest way to summarize the three parts of prophecy: *When God stops speaking, we should too!* People who are prophesying often feel the pressure to give an interpretation, particularly when the prophetic word seems ambiguous or even silly. It is astounding what some people think their prophetic words mean! The following is a profound example of a powerful prophetic word that was misinterpreted by the person who delivered it. Remember, we don't have to be profound to be powerful.

Some time ago several of us traveled to a Morning Star conference where they were training people how to prophesy. With about 70 people in the room, we were all prophesying to a woman in the front of the room. When we had completed the ten prophecies allowed each person, and began to judge the words given, a man in the back of the room stood to his feet and said, "You have on a yellow shirt!"

Immediately the woman fell to the ground, crying hysterically. The man continued to prophesy, saying things like, "The sun is yellow...the moon is yellow," and so on. When the woman finally regained her composure, the leader of the class asked her what that word meant to her.

She explained, "I have a son who is autistic and I told the Lord today, 'If you are going to heal my son, have someone tell me that I have on a yellow shirt....'"

Questions to Ponder

1. What is the difference between the gift of prophecy and the office of a prophet?

   _____

   _____

2. What is the difference between the gifts of the Spirit and the fruits of the Spirit?

   _____

   _____

3. Who can prophesy?

   _____

   _____

4. What are the three parts of prophecy?

   _____

   _____

5. What does the word *prophecy* mean?

   _____

   _____

Questions for Group Discussion

1. How can we tell what our giftings, callings, and annointings are?
2. What are the ramifications of getting identity from gifting instead of calling?

Life Application

Take time now with the Holy Spirit to discover what gifts the Lord has given you. Now ask Him for gifts that you have never walked in. Go to someone who is gifted in the area that you are asking God to gift you in, and have that person lay hands on you and pray for you to receive this gift. Go out and try it!

Let the journey begin!

Chapter 3

Learning to Hear the Voice of God

This chapter discusses why the voice of God can sometimes seem elusive or even nonexistent; and investigates the many sources of voices that speak to us from the spirit realm.

God Is Always Speaking

Jesus died on the Cross not just to forgive our sins but ultimately to bring us into a relationship with God. Communication is probably the single greatest vehicle of any relationship. Although some people have a problem believing that God wants to talk to everybody, most believers understand that true prayer is not just petitioning Heaven with a list of requests, but is communicating with Him as a true friend.

Jesus said, "*My sheep hear My voice...*" (John 10:27). Prophecy, in its simplest form is merely hearing from the Holy Spirit and repeating what He said. Paul said it this way, "*For you can all prophesy one by one...*" (1 Cor. 14:31). Moses said, "*Would that all the Lord's people were prophets, that the Lord would put His Spirit upon them!*" (Num. 11:29).

Knowledge is power. God doesn't want the prideful to be the powerful, therefore, God hides His Word so that only the hungry and the humble have access to His voice. God's Word is hidden from the arrogant and the proud.

At that very time He rejoiced greatly in the Holy Spirit, and said, "I praise You, O Father, Lord of Heaven and earth, that You have hidden these things from the wise and intelligent and have revealed them to infants. Yes, Father, for this way was well-pleasing in Your sight (Luke 10:21).

The Example of the Parables

The parables of Jesus are some of the best examples in Scripture of how the Lord conceals His treasures from the arrogant and proud. Many have been taught that Jesus told parables to demonstrate spiritual principles with natural illustrations. However, Jesus made it clear that He told parables so that people would *not* understand truth and become powerful. God does not want the prideful to be the powerful. Parables were told not to *reveal* truth, but to *hide* it.

And the disciples came and said to Him, "Why do You speak to them in parables?" Jesus answered them, "To you it has been granted to know the mysteries of the kingdom of heaven, but to them it has not been granted. For whoever has, to him more shall be given, and he will have an abundance; but whoever does not have, even what he has shall be taken away from him. Therefore I speak to them in parables; because while seeing they do not see, and while hearing they do not hear, nor do they understand" (Matthew 13:10-13).

But blessed are your eyes, because they see; and your ears, because they hear (Matthew 13:16).

Those who are hungry will search out the treasures that God has hidden for them. The Greek word for "hidden" is *langanw*, which means, "to be ignorant or unaware."

When we study the prophets of the Old Testament, we can easily become envious of how clearly they heard God's voice. However, Jesus makes it plain that those who are born again have a tremendous advantage over anyone who lived under the old covenant because God's Spirit now *resides **within*** us and is in constant communication with our spirit.

It is the glory of God to conceal a matter, but the glory of kings is to search out a matter (Proverbs 25:2).

For truly I say to you that many prophets and righteous men desired to see what you see, and did not see it, and to hear what you hear, and did not hear it (Matthew 13:17).

God's Goal Is Relationship

God does not want to simply impart information through the gift of prophecy, but rather the goal of all prophetic ministry is to draw us into a deeper relationship with Jesus and His Body. Malachi said that in the last days God would send Elijah the prophet and he will restore the hearts of the fathers to children and the hearts of the children to Father's (see Mal. 4:5-6).

Here again we see God's goal for the prophetic ministry deeply rooted in the restoration of relationships. Therefore, if we begin to use the gift of prophecy as a tool to expand our ministry rather than accepting it as an invitation to a deeper relationship with Jesus and His Church, He will "change His language" so that He can tutor us!

As He teaches us His new language, He creates an opportunity for us to draw closer to Himself and closer to His people.

> **God is always speaking, but His first language is not English.**

The Lord Is Always Speaking

The Lord is more determined and excited to speak to us than we are to hear from Him. We must realize that God is always speaking but He is *not human* and His first language is *not English!* If we can grasp this revelation and realize that most of us don't really know how well we see and hear God, we can begin to "tune our receivers to *His* station."

For example, in the room you are in right now there is music playing all around you. Even if you close your eyes and listen very carefully, you would not hear it. However, by simply *turning on a radio, you would perceive what was there all the time.* The reason, of course, is that our human bodies were never designed to perceive radio waves.

Likewise, God is always speaking to us! The gift of prophecy is the equipment we need to tap into the spirit realm that exists all around us even though we can't hear it with our naked ear. The gift of prophecy is like a radio receiver from Heaven. It gives us the ability to hear what God has been speaking to us all along but we were unable to perceive before we received this wonderful gift.

Anointing to Perceive the Supernatural

The king of Israel sent to the place about which the man of God had told him; thus he warned him, so that he guarded himself there, more than once or twice. Now the heart of the king of Aram was enraged over this thing; and he called his servants and said to them, "Will you tell me which of us is for the king of Israel?" One of his servants said, "No, my lord, O king; but Elisha, the prophet who is in Israel, tells the king of Israel the words that you speak in your bedroom." So he said, "Go and see where he is, that I may send and take him." And it was told him, saying, "Behold, he is in Dothan."

He sent horses and chariots and a great army there, and they came by night and surrounded the city. Now when the attendant of the man of God had risen early and gone out, behold, an army with horses and chariots was circling the city. And his servant said to him, "Alas, my master! What shall we do?" So he answered, "Do not fear, for those who are with us are more than those who are with them." Then Elisha prayed and said, "O Lord, I pray, open his eyes that he may see." And the Lord opened the servant's eyes and he saw; and behold, the mountain was full of horses and chariots of fire all around Elisha (2 Kings 6:10-17).

In Second Kings chapter 6, we see that Elisha's calling as a prophet gave him the ability to hear what King Aram would say in secret to his troops. Elisha became a secret weapon to the king of Israel by revealing the plans of this enemy. Then King Aram decides to capture Elisha. On the day of the attack, Elisha's servant comes out of the tent and sees that this enemy army has encircled them. In a panic, his servant runs into the tent and tells Elisha that they are in trouble. Elisha calmly prays for his servant. Immediately, the eyes of his attendant open and he realizes that the mountains are full of horses and chariots of God.

This is the kind of prophetic gift that each of us can receive from God. It causes us to be anointed to perceive what is *already happening in the spirit world*. Without this prophetic gift, we are like blind people in the Kingdom of God!

The War to Keep Us Deaf

Sometimes we struggle to hear the voice of God because there is a war to keep us spiritually deaf.

In the parable of the sower, Jesus explains why often when God speaks to us, the enemy comes along and tries to convince us that we didn't hear God clearly or that it wasn't God's voice at all! Satan's objective is to *prevent us from bringing God's comfort and encouragement to one another through the prophetic word.* If he can convince us not to speak the word of the Lord by making us feel foolish, or convince us that it was just our imagination and not a prophetic word, then he has succeeded in stealing the *fruit* of God's word in someone's life!

The sower sows the Word. These are the ones who are beside the road where the Word is sown; and when they hear, immediately Satan comes and takes away the Word which has been sown in them (Mark 4:14-15).

This principle is also true when it comes to *receiving* a prophetic word. If the enemy can persuade us that the word spoken to us wasn't really God, then we are robbed of the benefit! The value we place on the word will determine the power we will receive from it.

> **The value you place on the word determines the power you receive from it.**

Valuing the Prophetic Word

The Bible says, "*He who receives a prophet in the name of a prophet shall receive a prophet's reward*" (Matt. 10:41). What is a prophet's reward? *The ability to **see** and **hear**.* Jesus stood before a crowd and shouted, "*HE THAT HAS EYES LET HIM SEE, AND HE THAT HAS EARS LET HIM HEAR!*" He was acting as a prophet.

He who receives a prophet in the name of a prophet shall receive a prophet's reward; and he who receives a righteous man in the name of a righteous man shall receive a righteous man's reward (Matthew 10:41).

Everyone who valued Jesus as a prophet and received the words He shouted, received the ability to see and hear. A grace was released with His words that opened their eyes and ears!

*Gene and Lisa took us to lunch after I spoke at their church one Sunday. They had just adopted two boys after several years of trying to have children. During our meal together, the Lord spoke to me and said, "Tell Lisa that at this time next year she is going to have a baby." I argued with the Lord and told Him I didn't want to give her this word, knowing that she and Gene had received **lots** of prayer over the years about this issue. He said to me, "If you do not tell her, she will not get pregnant!"*

I obediently leaned toward Lisa and quietly told her what the Lord had spoken to me. Although they had been prayed for countless times over the years to conceive children, they received the word of the Lord and Lisa loudly announced, "I'M GOING TO HAVE A BABY!"

A few months later, we came home to a message on our answering machine from Lisa proudly proclaiming, "I'M PREGNANT!"

The next year she had a child, just as the Lord had promised.

Valuing the word of the Lord means that we make time to hear Him. Moses walked past the burning bush in the desert and heard nothing until he stopped and turned aside; we need to set aside time to diligently seek God ourselves with our whole heart.

The angel of the Lord appeared to him in a blazing fire from the midst of a bush; and he looked, and behold, the bush was burning with fire, yet the bush was not consumed. So Moses said, "I must turn aside now and see this marvelous sight, why the bush is not burned up." When the Lord saw that he turned aside to look, God called to him from the midst of the bush and said, "Moses, Moses!" And he said, "Here I am" (Exodus 3:2-4).

But from there you will seek the Lord your God, and you will find Him if you search for Him with all your heart and all your soul (Deuteronomy 4:29).

For the eyes of the Lord move to and fro throughout the earth that He may strongly support those whose heart is completely His. You have acted foolishly in this. Indeed, from now on you will surely have wars (2 Chronicles 16:9).

Even if God speaks audibly from Heaven, some people would only hear it as the sound of thunder. The difference between the deaf and the hearing is not how loud God speaks, but how open we are to hear Him speak.

"Father, glorify Your name." Then a voice came out of Heaven: "I have both glorified it, and will glorify it again." So the crowd of people who stood by and heard it were saying that it had thundered; others were saying, "An angel has spoken to Him" (John 12:28-29).

Testing the Spirits

As we are learning to hear the voice of the Holy Spirit, we must realize that not every voice that speaks to us from the spirit realm is from God.

Beloved, do not believe every spirit, but test the spirits to see whether they are from God, because many false prophets have gone out into the world (1 John 4:1).

In First John 4, we are instructed as *"the beloved"* to *"not believe every spirit, but test the spirits to see whether they are from God, because many false prophets have gone out into the world."* In this passage of Scripture, it is made clear that we—*the beloved*—are able to hear from spirits *other* than the *Holy Spirit* and are warned not to become false prophets by *listening to the wrong spirit*! Therefore, if it is *possible* to become a false prophet by listening to the wrong spirit, then it becomes vital to know *which* voices can speak to us.

Who Is Speaking to Us?

Voices that speak to us from the spirit realm come from four sources:

1. Our spirit.

2. The Holy Spirit.

3. Evil spirits.

4. Angels.

The Four Sources

Our spirit: We are a spirit that has a soul and a body. When we are born again, our spirit comes to life making it possible to hear from the spirit realm, but not necessarily hearing from the Holy Spirit. Hearing from our own spirit is still a spiritual experience and being aware of this will help us discern which voice is speaking to us.

The Holy Spirit: This is God's Spirit, the one who we are building a relationship with and learning to hear clearly.

Evil spirits: Spirits from the evil realm can speak to Christians just as they spoke to Jesus when He encountered satan in the wilderness.

Angels: According to Hebrews chapter 1, these are spirits sent to render service to the saints. Angels also speak to us about the things of God.

Practice Makes Perfect

In the following chapters, there is a more thorough discussion about how to recognize which spirit you are hearing. It takes time to learn to discern what spirit is speaking to you and there is no substitute for experience.

A banker who had reached the age of retirement was about to be replaced by a young man. Upon his arrival to take the helm from his predecessor, he asked the older man how he became successful. The man replied, "*Good decisions.*"

"How do you make good decisions?" the young man asked.

"*Experience,*" the banker replied.

The young man thought for a moment, and then inquired, "How do you get experience?"

With a warm smile aged with wisdom, he replied, "Bad decisions!"

You cannot grow in the gifts of the Spirit without making mistakes! We gain experience as we step out in faith trying to listen to the Holy Spirit.

Many years ago I went fishing with a man who was several years my senior. We stood on the same bank, using the same bait, and I watched as he caught several fish while I was unsuccessful. Certain that the problem was the pole I was using, I asked if we could swap equipment and he graciously traded poles with me. Still I caught nothing, as he continued to reel in more fish!

I finally decided that the only fish I was going to catch that day was one that was going to commit suicide. He knew what the problem was, but it took me a while to realize that I did not know how it felt to get a bite.

You see, the old man had experience.

Questions to Ponder

1. List four reasons why we sometimes don't hear God's voice.

    _____

    _____

2. Why does God sometimes change His language?

    _____

    _____

3. What is the main factor in hearing from God?

    _____

    _____

4. How does satan affect our ability to hear God?

    _____

    _____

Questions for Group Discussion

1. How are risk and faith related?
2. How does this affect our prophetic ability?

Life Application

Having a pure heart is vitally important in communicating with God. The pure in heart see God. Take some time now to ask the Lord to search your heart. Let humility and hunger be your guide.

Chapter 4

The Language of God

This chapter is dedicated to understanding the different ways in which God communicates with His people. God's first language is not English. How then does God speak to us? You may be surprised!

Visions and Dreams

One of the most common ways the Lord communicates with us is through visions and dreams.

"And it shall be in the last days," God says, "that I will pour forth of My Spirit on all mankind; and your sons and your daughters shall prophesy, and your young men shall see visions, and your old men shall dream dreams; even on my bondslaves, both men and women, I will in those days pour forth of My Spirit and they shall prophesy" (Acts 2:17-18).

Visions

There are two types of visions. The first one is a *Vision of the Mind*, in which the Lord "projects" images and pictures onto the "screen" of our minds. This can be called a "sanctified imagination" or an imagination that is under the influence of the Holy Spirit. Most often, this is how the Holy Spirit speaks to us.

For example, if you were asked to picture a pink elephant, you would see it in your mind's eye. The Holy Spirit uses your mind as a blackboard in which He draws pictures or projects images onto your mind's eye.

The second type of vision is an *Open Vision*. This is an image that you see with your natural eyes. The following is an example of an open vision.

Many years ago, I took a group of about 37 kids from our youth group to Santa Cruz, California, for a day on the beach. Among them was our foster daughter, Dee. It happened to be "Muscle Beach Day" and the area was overflowing with people. Our group found a spot to settle and enjoy the day.

Not long after our arrival, I glanced up and saw Dee running along the beach being chased by a man dressed in full leathers. As they ran toward us, I could hear the man shouting to Dee, "I love you! I love you! I'm taking you with me."

She ran to me for protection with this man close behind her. As she knelt next to me in the sand, he reached over and grabbed her by the blouse. He began to shake her, saying loudly, "I love you! I love you!"

Finally, I mustered the courage to grab the man's arm. "That's enough!" I yelled. The man abruptly dropped Dee in the sand, then turned and grabbed me, lifting me up off my knees! He screamed at me, "I love her! I'm taking her with me!"

Just then I saw an open vision appear above his head. Events of his life flashed over him in what appeared to be short video clips! I said to him, "Your mother is in the hospital dying, isn't she?"

"Yes!" he exclaimed.

"Your dad died last year, didn't he?" I shouted.

"Yea," he said.

Then I yelled, "And you blame yourself, don't you?"

With a look of shock and disbelief he said, "Man, you're scaring me!" He turned around and ran away.

I jumped to my feet and chased after him! The whole event turned into quite a scene for the other beachgoers as I caught up with him and tackled him three times. Each time I tackled him, I yelled "YOU NEED JESUS!"

"I know!" he yelled back.

The outrageous event ended when he turned and ran toward his motorcycle gang. He stopped about a hundred yards from me, turned and shouted, "You pray for me!"

"What's your name?"

He shouted back, "Phillip."

Dreams

Dreams are also the language of the Holy Spirit. There are two types of dreams. The first is what could be called a *Virtual Reality Dream*. This occurs while we sleep and remains in our mind after waking.

The following is an example of a virtual reality dream that Nebuchadnezzar had in the days of Daniel. Notice that the dream is symbolic and needs an interpretation.

You, O king, were looking and behold, there was a single great statue; that statue, which was large and of extraordinary splendor, was standing in front of you, and its appearance was awesome. The head of that statue was made of fine gold, its breast and its arms of silver, its belly and its thighs of bronze, its legs of iron, its feet partly of iron and partly of clay. You continued looking until a stone was cut out without hands, and it struck the statue on its feet of iron and clay and crushed them. Then the iron, the clay, the bronze, the silver and the gold were crushed all at the same time and became like chaff from the summer threshing floors; and the wind carried them away so that not a trace of them was found. But the stone that struck the statue became a great mountain and filled the whole earth (Daniel 2:31-35).

The second type of dream can be called a *Reality Dream*. This is a real experience we have while sleeping that we remember after waking. The spirit world never sleeps. Therefore, our spirit can interact with the spirit world while our soul sleeps. An example of this type of dream is found in Genesis chapter 20, where it states, "*God came to Abimelech in a dream.*"

Notice in this reality dream it *does not* say that he *dreamt* of God, but rather that he had a *real encounter with the Lord* and that he remembered it when he woke up.

But God came to Abimelech in a dream of the night, and said to him, "Behold, you are a dead man because of the woman whom you have taken, for she is married" (Genesis 20:3).

Another example of a *Reality Dream* is in the familiar story of Joseph in Matthew chapter 2. In this event, an angel of the Lord interacts with Joseph while he sleeps.

Now when they had gone, behold, an angel of the Lord appeared to Joseph in a dream and said, "Get up! Take the Child and His mother and flee to Egypt, and remain there until I tell you; for Herod is going to search for the Child to destroy Him" (Matthew 2:13).

Dreams are multifaceted and have many purposes. The Book of Job speaks of dreams that keep us from hell.

Indeed God speaks once, or twice, yet no one notices it. In a dream, a vision of the night, when sound sleep falls on men, while they slumber in their beds, then He opens the ears of men, and seals their instruction, that He may turn man aside from his conduct, and keep man from pride; He keeps back his soul from the pit, and his life from passing over into Sheol (Job 33:14-18).

A friend of ours told us how his son's marriage was restored because of a dream! The night before they were to go to divorce court, his daughter-in-law had a dream. In it she saw the Lord hugging her husband and father-in-law in a field of flowers while she looked on from a distance. In the next scene, she saw herself standing in the field of flowers with Jesus walking toward her. When He reached out to embrace her, she woke up. The next morning, she knew that the Lord wanted her to restore her relationship with her husband. She reconciled their marriage that very day!

According to Joseph in the Book of Genesis, a dream that has been repeated twice means that the matter is determined by God and adjustments in your life are needed to accommodate what is about to take place.

Now as for the repeating of the dream to Pharaoh twice, it means that the matter is determined by God, and God will quickly bring it about (Genesis 41:32).

Important things to remember about dreams.

1. Not all dreams are from God. As we learned earlier, we can hear from all four sources of the spirit realm, even in our dreams.

2. Simply because we have powerful and illustrative dreams does not necessarily mean we are prophetic. Remember that wicked people in the Old Testament had dreams. Interpreting dreams is what makes us prophetic.

3. Colors, numbers, and other symbolic occurrences in dreams are very important to the interpretation of the dream. Ultimately the interpretation of dreams belongs to the Lord.

4. A good way for us to increase our supernatural dream life is to lay a notebook or tape recorder by our bed before going to sleep. Pray to the Lord and tell Him, "*Your servant is listening.*" As soon as you have a dream, write it down or record all of the details that you can remember including the way you felt about the dream while you were having it.

However, there is a God in heaven who reveals mysteries, and He has made known to King Nebuchadnezzar what will take place in the latter days. This was your dream and the visions in your mind while on your bed (Daniel 2:28).

Communicating With God

God's Still Small Voice

At times, the Lord speaks to us in a still small voice from within our spirit. This can be heard as a passing thought, sudden impression, or internal "sense" of something that God is saying. This still small voice is illustrated in the Book of First Kings. In this account, God is not in the strong wind or the earthquake, but rather He is in the gentle blowing.

So He said, "Go forth and stand on the mountain before the Lord." And behold, the Lord was passing by! And a great and strong wind was rending the mountains and breaking in pieces the rocks before the Lord; but the Lord was not in the wind. And after the wind an earthquake, but the Lord was not in the earthquake. After the

earthquake a fire, but the Lord was not in the fire; and after the fire a sound of a gentle blowing. When Elijah heard it, he wrapped his face in his mantle and went out and stood in the entrance of the cave. And behold, a voice came to him and said, "What are you doing here, Elijah?" (1 Kings 19:11-13).

Angels

Angels are another voice from the heavenly realm. Throughout the New Testament angels visited and spoke to people concerning what they should do.

But an angel of the Lord spoke to Philip saying, "Get up and go south to the road that descends from Jerusalem to Gaza" (Acts 8:26).

On the very night when Herod was about to bring him forward, Peter was sleeping between two soldiers, bound with two chains, and guards in front of the door were watching over the prison. And behold, an angel of the Lord suddenly appeared and a light shone in the cell; and he struck Peter's side and woke him up, saying, "Get up quickly." And his chains fell off his hands (Acts 12:6-7).

Trances

Trances are another way that God speaks to His people. Trances are much like visions, except that when we are in a trance, we are completely unaware of our surroundings. The Greek word for *trance* means "to be out of your mind." Trances take us out of our natural minds and into God's. Many Christians feel that because people in the occult have trances, all trances are from the devil. The truth is, satan can only *copy* the things of God.

On the next day, as they were on their way and approaching the city, Peter went up on the housetop about the sixth hour to pray. But he became hungry and was desiring to eat; but while they were making preparations, he fell into a trance; and he saw the sky opened up, and an object like a great sheet coming down, lowered by four corners to the ground (Acts 10:9-11).

Creation

Creation itself is a voice from the Lord and speaks to us in many ways. The obvious way is that God's creation tells us about who God is. The mountains speak of His strength, the rivers of His provision and the flowers of His beauty. Another way creation speaks to us is by God actually *causing nature to do things that are prophetic acts.*

For since the creation of the world His invisible attributes, His eternal power and divine nature, have been clearly seen, being understood through what has been made, so that they are without excuse (Romans 1:20).

One year, every time Bethel church would meet to pray, a roadrunner would show up outside the glass door with a lizard in its mouth! This went on for months until we finally realized that the Lord was calling us to go out to the roads, the highways, and the byways and compel the lost to come in! He was literally calling us to evangelism!

One day the roadrunner managed to find his way inside the church. In a desperate attempt to get out of the building, he hit a window and died. I believe the Lord showed us through this event that if we did not reach out to the lost that our church would die.

Scriptures

The Lord can speak to us in our daily reading of the Bible. He can also highlight a verse or story that speaks to us about our circumstance. Sometimes God will even use a Scripture out of context! We must be careful, however, that although a verse may be out of context but still speak to us, it should never violate the overall guidelines of the Scripture.

All Scripture is inspired by God and profitable for teaching, for reproof, for correction, for training in righteousness; so that the man of God may be adequate, equipped for every good work (2 Timothy 3:16-17).

Tongues

Tongues and the interpretation of tongues are both a gift from God and a voice from Heaven. Notice that the Lord calls it the *interpretation* of tongues—not the *translation* of tongues. In other words, the tongue can be quite lengthy while the interpretation of it brief or vice versa. If you like to have things your own way, I suggest you don't pray in tongues! For example, if we were to pray in English, asking the Lord for a Corvette, then start to pray in tongues, the Holy Spirit could be praying, "Lord don't give them a Corvette! They will hurt themselves in that car!"

For to one is given the word of wisdom through the Spirit, and to another the word of knowledge according to the same Spirit; to another faith by the same Spirit, and to another gifts of healing by the one Spirit, and to another the effecting of miracles, and to another prophecy, and to another the distinguishing of spirits, to another various kinds of tongues, and to another the interpretation of tongues (1 Corinthians 12:8-10).

Impressions

Many prophetic people experience discernment through impressions without even realizing it. Oftentimes we can sense an evil spirit on someone just by sitting down next to that person. The evil spirit that is troubling the person who is next to us will begin to trouble us in the same manner. For instance, if a spirit of fear troubles a person in a close geographic area, we can actually begin to feel fearful as well. If we do not realize our prophetic ability and discernment in this area, we can begin to feel very confused or think we are crazy. Within this viewpoint, it is possible that those diagnosed as "bipolar" may actually be experiencing a powerful level of discernment, but do not, unfortunately, know how to use this gift properly.

...and to another the effecting of miracles, and to another prophecy, and to another the distinguishing of spirits, to another various kinds of tongues, and to another the interpretation of tongues (1 Corinthians 12:10).

Prophetic Acts

Oftentimes the Lord will direct someone to do a prophetic act, as in the following Scripture example. This was common in the Bible. Jeremiah set a brick in the middle of the city—a prophetic symbol of laying a siege wall against Israel. Agabus tied a belt around himself as a way of showing Paul how he would suffer.

And coming to us, he took Paul's belt and bound his own feet and hands, and said, "This is what the Holy Spirit says: 'In this way the Jews at Jerusalem will bind the man who owns this belt and deliver him into the hands of the Gentiles'" (Acts 21:11).

Signs and Wonders

Many times God will perform signs and wonders as a way to communicate His love or direction.

So Gideon said to Him, "If now I have found favor in Your sight, then show me a sign that it is You who speak with me. Please do not depart from here, until I come back to You, and bring out my offering and lay it before You." And He said, "I will remain until you return." Then Gideon went in and prepared a young goat and unleavened bread from an ephah of flour; he put the meat in a basket and the broth in a pot, and brought them out to him under the oak and presented them. The angel of God said to him, "Take the meat and the unleavened bread and lay them on this rock, and pour out the broth." And he did so. Then the angel of the Lord put out the end of the staff that was in his hand and touched the meat and the unleavened bread; and fire sprang up from the rock and consumed the meat and the unleavened bread. Then the angel of the Lord vanished from his sight (Judges 6:17-21).

Mind Reading

Jesus demonstrated this prophetic ability over and over again in His ministry. He would answer questions that no one asked because He knew what was on their minds.

But He knew their thoughts *and said to them, "Any kingdom divided against itself is laid waste; and a house divided against itself falls"* (Luke 11:17, emphasis added).

There are times when someone is ministering to a person prophetically and can read that person's thoughts. Not realizing what just took place, the person ministering may begin to prophesy to the person receiving ministry their desires instead of the heart of the Lord. Understanding that prophetic people can sometimes read the minds of others helps to keep this dynamic out of our prophecies.

Circumstances

God can speak to us and direct us through the circumstances of our lives. This dynamic occurs as God opens and closes the doors of opportunity. It is easy to misunderstand this principle and think that any time we come up against an obstacle in our life that God cannot be in it. However, keep in mind that any time we are doing something for God, the devil will oppose us!

I know your deeds. Behold, I have put before you an open door which no one can shut, because you have a little power, and have kept My word, and have not denied My name (Revelation 3:8).

Dance

Many churches have dancers as part of their worship team. Oftentimes, God will begin to choreograph a supernatural, spontaneous dance, which is actually a prophetic act that the Lord is speaking to us through the dance.

Then the virgin will rejoice in the dance, and the young men and the old, together, for I will turn their mourning into joy and will comfort them and give them joy for their sorrow (Jeremiah 31:13).

Prophetic Songs

Often during worship the Lord will give someone a spontaneous song that is from God to the people. It is common for God to give the prophetic singer the lyrics and the melody.

Let the Word of Christ richly dwell within you, with all wisdom teaching and admonishing one another with psalms and hymns and spiritual songs, singing with thankfulness in your hearts to God (Colossians 3:16).

Prophetic Body Checks

Sometimes the Lord will communicate His desire to heal someone else's body by causing pain or a sensation in a certain part of the prophetic person's body; it typically correlates to the sickness in the person that God wants to heal. If we receive this kind of information from the Holy Spirit, it is important that we are aware of what pain or discomfort is common to us. Without clarification, we could mistakenly confuse our pain with a word of knowledge for healing.

Spiritual Happenings

Spiritual happenings are another way that God speaks to us. These are supernatural *incidents* that correlate with *natural* events. Notice that in the Book of Numbers, Aaron's rod came alive after being dead, and bore blossoms and ripe almonds as a sign from God that he was anointed to be a leader of Israel.

Speak to the sons of Israel, and get from them a rod for each father's household: twelve rods, from all their leaders according to their fathers' households. You shall write each name on his rod, and write Aaron's name on the rod of Levi; for there is one rod for the head of each of their fathers' households. You shall then deposit them in the tent of meeting in front of the testimony, where I meet with you. It will come about that the rod of the man whom I choose will sprout. Thus I will lessen from upon Myself the grumblings of the sons of Israel, who are grumbling against you.

Moses therefore spoke to the sons of Israel, and all their leaders gave him a rod apiece, for each leader according to their fathers' households, twelve rods, with the rod of Aaron among their rods. So Moses deposited the rods before the Lord in the tent of the testimony. Now on the next day Moses went into the tent of the testimony; and behold, the rod of Aaron for the house of Levi had sprouted and put forth buds and produced blossoms, and it bore ripe almonds (Numbers 17:2-8).

Some time ago, every time I entered a worship service, I noticed that my watch gained an hour. After purchasing three different watches, all of which gained an hour only during worship, I finally asked the Lord what this could mean.

He said, "It's later than you think."

Questions to Ponder

1. What is one way to increase our dream life?

   _____

   _____

2. How is the discerning of spirits a voice from God?

   _____

   _____

3. What is one of the most common mistakes people make when they allow God to direct them through circumstances?

   _____

   _____

4. Name two ways that creation can speak to us.

   _____

   _____

5. What is the difference between a vision and a trance?

   _____

   _____

Questions for Group Discussion

1. What is the most common way in which God speaks to you personally?

2. Is there anything that has occurred in your life that, after reading this chapter, you realize now was a voice from God?

Life Application

Go on a Holy Spirit adventure! You can do this by simply taking a few minutes to pray and ask the Holy Spirit to show you where to go and who to talk to. He is eager to accompany you on this exploit. You will learn how to hear His voice—be ready for some surprises along the way!

Chapter 5

Judging and Receiving Prophetic Words

Developing a safe environment for the gifts of the spirit to operate effectively is important. This chapter examines the reasons why prophecy needs to be judged and the proper criteria by which prophetic ministry should be evaluated. We will also explore the correct way to receive prophetic words.

Judge All Prophecy

In First Thessalonians, Paul instructs us not to despise prophetic utterances. Any of us who have had experience with prophetic ministry can easily understand why Paul would bring up the subject of *despising prophetic* ministry. Many churches, in response to poor prophetic ministry, have altogether eliminated the gifts of the Spirit from their services and teachings. We also learn that a prophetic word should be examined carefully, and that we should hold on to what is found to be good.

Do not quench the Spirit; do not despise prophetic utterances. But examine everything carefully; hold fast to that which is good (1 Thessalonians 5:19-21).

Paul's exhortation, however, is that the Kingdom of God does not consist of words but of power (see 1 Cor. 4:20). He also reminds us, *"that your faith should not rest on the wisdom of man, but on the power of God"* (1 Cor. 2:5).

Prophets Can Make Mistakes Without Being False Prophets

"Let two or three prophets speak, and let the others pass judgment" (1 Corinthians 14:29).

Many people in the church have a problem believing that a real prophet of God can make a *mistake* while prophesying. They assume only *false prophets* make mistakes. In First Corinthians, we are exhorted to let two or three prophets speak in a service and to let the other prophets offer judgment on the word.

The truth is that even the apostles and prophets in the Bible gave prophecies that were not entirely accurate.

One example is in Acts 21. Agabus the prophet prophesied that the Jews in Jerusalem would bind Paul and hand him over to the Gentiles.

As we were staying there for some days, a prophet named Agabus came down from Judea. And coming to us, he took Paul's belt and bound his own feet and hands, and said, "This is what the Holy Spirit says: 'In this way the Jews at Jerusalem will bind the man who owns this belt and deliver him into the hands of the Gentiles'" (Acts 21:10-11).

What *actually* happened: the Gentiles *rescued* Paul from the Jews.

At once he took along some soldiers and centurions and ran down to them; and when they saw the commander and the soldiers, they stopped beating Paul. Then the commander came up and took hold of him, and ordered him to be bound with chains; and he began asking who he was and what he had done (Acts 21:32-33).

In verse 30 of Acts chapter 22, the commander turned Paul over to the Jews. This was the *opposite* of what Agabus prophesied.

But on the next day, wishing to know for certain why he had been accused by the Jews, he released him and ordered the chief priests and all the council to assemble, and brought Paul down and set him before him (Acts 22:30).

It is obvious that Agabus was correct about the *heart* of what God was saying, but he got the details slightly mixed up.

Another example of a prophetic word that was not entirely accurate can be found in Acts 27:10. Here Paul says, in essence, *"If we sail on, we will lose the ship and we will all die."* However, later in verses 22 and 23 of that Acts chapter 27, Paul is *corrected* by an angel who says, "*There will be no loss of life, but only of the ship.*" This may seem like a minor mistake unless you happen to be one of the men on the ship!

Theologically, some people quote Deuteronomy chapter 18 as evidence that a prophet is false if some of their prophecies are inaccurate. We need to understand the difference between the Old Testament and New Testament prophetic ministry.

I will raise up a prophet from among their countrymen like you, and I will put My words in his mouth, and he shall speak to them all that I command (Deuteronomy 18:18).

But the prophet who speaks a word presumptuously in My name which I have not commanded him to speak, or which he speaks in the name of other gods, that prophet shall die (Deuteronomy 18:20).

Old Testament Versus New Testament Prophecy

In the Old Testament, prophets *received* the word of the Lord.

In the New Testament, prophetic people *perceive* the word of the Lord.

In the Old Testament, the Spirit of God did not live inside of man, nor had the spirit of man been brought to life. This happens during the new birth process when we receive Christ. Therefore, when a prophet in the Old Testament heard from God, it was an occasion because Christ was not living inside of them.

In this new dispensation, our spirit is alive and the Holy Spirit lives inside of us. Now, as Christians, we daily interact with the spirit world. It is easy to confuse the Holy Spirit's words with our newly regenerated spirit's words. Remember, now we can have a spiritual experience without the Holy Spirit's participation for *we are a spirit trying to have a temporary, human experience.*

The reason why prophecy in the Old Testament was not judged (except to kill the prophet or to wait to see if the prophecy would come to pass) is because the people were spiritually dead. They had no spiritual paradigm by which to process spiritual information. In those days, their judgment was based on whether or not they *liked* the word. It is easy to see why, in the Old Testament, they killed prophets who misled them. These men had tremendous influence over their people, as well as countries.

In the New Testament church, however, the Christian who receives the word has as much responsibility to judge the word as the one who *gave* it because *both the giver and receiver have the same Holy Spirit living inside of them.*

Developing a Refuse Gate

Some people are overly sensitive to negative spiritual experiences. They spend their lives trying to stay safe and clean. God has made His people durable. In the city of Jerusalem there was a refuse gate—the area where all of the city garbage was dumped. Our own human body has a system of elimination that disposes of anything that does not nourish it. There is a need in the Body of Christ for a system of elimination as well. Otherwise, we will be poisoned by poor ministry or worse yet, starved to death by those who refuse the Holy Spirit's work because they are afraid that someone might "slime" them.

Order in the Church

The Bible tells us that the gifts of the Spirit should be practiced properly and in order. The first part of this commandment is that they should be practiced! There is no need for order if you never allow the Spirit to move. If you have ever witnessed the birth of a child, you will realize that God's idea of "decently and in order" is far different than ours. New life can be messy!

But all things must be done properly and in an orderly manner (1 Corinthians 14:40).

Wherever people are ministering to one another there will be messes. Messes are one of the signs that life is happening. The most orderly place on the planet is the graveyard; but there is no life there.

Where no oxen are, the manger is clean, but much revenue comes by the strength of the ox (Proverbs 14:4).

Think of what the manger is full of when there is much increase!

This does not mean that allowing the manifestation of the gifts of the Spirit in the church should be without guidelines. Jesus said that He pours new wine into new wineskins. He did not say that He pours new wine into no wineskins. In First Corinthians chapter 14, Paul instructs us to have order in the church. He tells us, *"the spirits of prophets are subject to prophets"* (1 Cor. 14:32). This means that no one can say that the Holy Spirit made him or her act in a disruptive manner. The Holy Spirit subjects Himself to us.

It is the responsibility of the church leadership to establish guidelines and boundaries. *When this is done, the Spirit will move inside of these when He is invited to.* This becomes the new wineskin, which of course must be *flexible*.

Guidelines for Judging Prophetic Words

1. The word must be congruent with the Scriptures as well as the heart of Father God.

But even if we, or an angel from heaven, should preach to you a gospel contrary to what we have preached to you, he is to be accursed! (Galatians 1:8).

2. It must bear witness with the spirit of the one who receives it.

The Spirit Himself testifies with our spirit that we are children of God (Romans 8:16).

3. The fruit of the prophetic word must be that the person receiving it is brought closer to God and His people.

More than that, I count all things to be loss in view of the surpassing value of knowing Christ Jesus my Lord, for whom I have suffered the loss of all things, and count them but rubbish so that I may gain Christ, and may be found in Him, not having a righteousness of my own derived from the Law, but that which is through faith in Christ, the righteousness which comes from God on the basis of faith, that I may

know Him and the power of His resurrection and the fellowship of His sufferings, being conformed to His death... (Philippians 3:8-10).

4. The prophets and leadership should be in agreement with the word and its interpretation and application.

Obey your leaders and submit to them, for they keep watch over your souls as those who will give an account. Let them do this with joy and not with grief, for this would be unprofitable for you (Hebrews 13:17).

5. The interpretation of any prophetic revelation belongs to God, not to man. Therefore, we also need the Holy Spirit's anointing to know the meaning of the word as well as what to do with it.

But know this first of all, that no prophecy of Scripture is a matter of one's own interpretation, for no prophecy was ever made by an act of human will, but men moved by the Holy Spirit spoke from God (2 Peter 1:20-21).

Sometimes when we receive a prophetic word, we don't realize what it means until after it has been fulfilled. An example of this is found in Exodus chapter 3 where Moses asks God for a sign so he can know for sure that it is God who is sending him. The Lord spoke to him and said, "*After you bring the people out of Egypt, you will worship at this mountain.*"

But Moses said to God, "Who am I, that I should go to Pharaoh, and that I should bring the sons of Israel out of Egypt?" And He said, "Certainly I will be with you, and this shall be the sign to you that it is I who have sent you: when you have brought the people out of Egypt, you shall worship God at this mountain" (Exodus 3:11-12).

Jesus' prophecy about His own death and resurrection was not understood until after He rose from the dead.

Jesus answered them, "Destroy this temple, and in three days I will raise it up." The Jews then said, "It took forty-six years to build this temple, and will You raise it up in three days?" But He was speaking of the temple of His body. So when He was raised from the dead, His disciples remembered that He said this; and they believed the Scripture and the word which Jesus had spoken (John 2:19-22).

Judging the Interpretation

It is easy to misjudge a prophetic word by believing that it relates to our *immediate* circumstances or something close to our heart that we are hoping for. This can be called *selective hearing*!

I have given hundreds of prophetic words to people over the years and I am sometimes amazed at what people *think* they hear me say. Occasionally, what people hear from prophecy and what the actual word is *are not even close* to the same thing!

A vivid example of this sort of misinterpretation is in the account of Matthew chapter 16. The disciples had neglected to bring bread. When Jesus says to them, "*Watch out and beware of the leaven of the Pharisees and Sadducees,*" they thought He was scolding them for forgetting the bread. How did they get that from the word, "*Beware of the leaven of the Pharisees and Sadducees?*" They read their circumstances into His word!

And Jesus said to them, "Watch out and beware of the leaven of the Pharisees and Sadducees." They began to discuss this among themselves, saying, "He said that because we did not bring any bread." But Jesus, aware of this, said, "You men of little faith, why do you discuss among yourselves that you have no bread? Do you not yet understand or remember the five loaves of the five thousand, and how many baskets full you picked up? Or the seven loaves of the four thousand, and how many large baskets full you picked up?"

"How is it that you do not understand that I did not speak to you concerning bread? But beware of the leaven of the Pharisees and Sadducees." Then they understood that He did not say to beware of the leaven of bread, but of the teaching of the Pharisees and Sadducees (Matthew 16:6-12).

Looking Into the Heart of the Matter

In the Book of Exodus, God tells Moses that He is going to kill the people that Moses led out of Egypt because they are obstinate and evil. Moses argues with the Lord that they are the Lord's people He led out of Egypt. After a long debate, God changes His mind and leads the people into the Promised Land. Why would God prophesy to Moses something He didn't really want to do? *Sometimes when God speaks to us, He is testing our hearts more than He is determining our destiny.* God was determining if Moses had the heart it would take to lead His people.

So the Lord changed His mind about the harm which He said He would do to His people (Exodus 32:14).

Sometimes when God speaks He is testing our hearts rather than revealing our destinies.

Traditionally, the church has had a single dimensional way to judge prophecy. But God is calling us into a deeper relationship with Him. This will lead us into new ways of judging prophetic ministry.

The Lord said to Moses, "I have seen this people, and behold, they are an obstinate people. Now then let Me alone, that My anger may burn against them and that I may destroy them; and I will make of you a great nation."

Then Moses entreated the Lord his God, and said, "O Lord, why does Your anger burn against Your people whom You have brought out from the land of Egypt with great power and with a mighty hand? Why should the Egyptians speak, saying, 'With evil intent He brought them out to kill them in the mountains and to destroy them from the face of the earth'? Turn from Your burning anger and change Your mind about doing harm to Your people. Remember Abraham, Isaac, and Israel, Your servants to whom You swore by Yourself, and said to them, 'I will multiply your descendants as the stars of the heavens, and all this land of which I have spoken I will give to your descendants, and they shall inherit it forever.'"

So the Lord changed His mind about the harm which He said He would do to His people (Exodus 32:9-14).

Here is another example of prophetic ministry that was received in an unusual manner.

Referring again to Agabus the prophet, he ministers to the apostle Paul by telling him that if he goes to Jerusalem he will be bound and arrested. Paul doesn't think the prophetic word means that God doesn't want him to go, but rather that God is telling him to count the cost. This emphasizes the need to look into the heart of God to truly understand what He wants instead of what He *seems* to be saying.

As we were staying there for some days, a prophet named Agabus came down from Judea. And coming to us, he took Paul's belt and bound his own feet and hands, and said, "This is what the Holy Spirit says: 'In this way the Jews at Jerusalem will bind the man who owns this belt and deliver him into the hands of the Gentiles.'"

When we had heard this, we as well as the local residents began begging him not to go up to Jerusalem. Then Paul answered, "What are you doing, weeping and breaking my heart? For I am ready not only to be bound, but even to die at Jerusalem for the name of the Lord Jesus" (Acts 21:10-13).

How to Receive Prophetic Words

When we are given a prophetic word, we must judge the word to make sure it is from God. The next step is for us to learn how to receive the word. It is important to know when to *get out of the way* and when to *prepare the way*. This point is illustrated in the life of Abraham and Sarah in Genesis chapters 16-21. God told them that they were going to have a son. But the years rolled on and still they had no children. Unfortunately, they decided to *help* God bring about His promise by having Abraham sleep with Hagar, Sarah's maid. This resulted in Hagar giving birth to Ishmael. Ishmael persecuted the child of promise the rest of his days (see Gal. 4:29).

Finally God came to Abraham and Sarah and prophesied to them that they were going to have a son the following year. Sarah laughed and said, *"After I have become old, shall I have pleasure, my lord being old also?"* (Gen. 18:12). But despite her doubt, Isaac was born the following year. The amazing thing to remember here is that Isaac was not born through immaculate conception. Abraham and Sarah had to participate in the union of marriage in order to have Isaac. In one respect, they created an Ishmael by trying to make the prophetic word come to pass, yet they still had to co-labor with God to see His promise become a reality.

We need to realize that God seldom does things all by Himself. He often requires us to be involved with Him to see our destinies fulfilled. The key here is to allow the Holy Spirit to show us what part He wants us to play and what part God has reserved for Himself. Otherwise, we will create Ishmaels who will persecute our Isaacs!

We also need to learn how to receive prophetic ministry multidimensionally. In other words, when God speaks to us about doing something new, He doesn't necessarily want us to stop our current activity. Usually, He wants to add to our responsibilities. This is illustrated in the parable of the talents. When the stewards were faithful with few talents, they received more for they had carefully tended what they had been given. We need to be careful how we apply prophetic words to our lives because God wants to bless us abundantly.

To one he gave five talents, to another, two, and to another, one, each according to his own ability; and he went on his journey. Immediately the one who had received the five talents went and traded with them, and gained five more talents. In the same manner the one who had received the two talents gained two more. But he who received the one talent went away, and dug a hole in the ground and hid his master's money.

Now after a long time the master of those slaves came and settled accounts with them. The one who had received the five talents came up and brought five more talents, saying, "Master, you entrusted five talents to me. See, I have gained five more talents." His master said to him, "Well done, good and faithful slave. You were faithful with a few things, I will put you in charge of many things; enter into the joy of your master." Also the one who had received the two talents came up and said, "Master, you entrusted two talents to me. See, I have gained two more talents." His master said to him, "Well done, good and faithful slave. You were faithful with a few things, I will put you in charge of many things; enter into the joy of your master" (Matthew 25:15-23).

Questions to Ponder

1. What is the difference between Old Testament and New Testament prophecy?

   _____

   _____

2. How is it possible to have a prophetic word from God that may have parts of it that are inaccurate?

   _____

   _____

3. Is it possible for a word to be scriptural but not from God? (Refer to Luke 4.)

   _____

   _____

4. Name the five ways that prophecy is to be judged.

   _____

   _____

Discussion Questions

1. What are some of the ways that we should work with people who continually give inaccurate words?

2. What should we do if we give a prophetic word to someone in our leadership and they believe the word is wrong even though we believe we heard from God?

Life Application

Team up with a couple of other prophetic people. Prophesy and give words of knowledge to each other. Ask those who received the words to judge them for accuracy. This is not the time to extend mercy to each other! Honesty is very important as we learn to hear the Holy Spirit's voice. We learn just as much from being wrong as we do from being right. So if the word that we received was not accurate, it is right and proper to tell the person who prophesied. We should also include the reason why we do not believe the word, or portions of it, are from God.

Chapter 6

Receiving and Ministering in the Gift of Prophecy

The previous chapters explored the Gift of Prophecy and how to allow the
Holy Spirit to flow through your life. This chapter reveals how
to receive and grow in the Holy Spirit's gifts.

How to Receive

The *most common* way to receive spiritual gifts is by having someone who is already gifted
lay hands on you and pray for an impartation of the gift or gifts of the Holy Spirit.

*For I long to see you so that I may impart some spiritual gift to you, that you may be
established* (Romans 1:11).

*And when Paul had laid his hands upon them, the Holy Spirit came on them, and
they began speaking with tongues and prophesying* (Acts 19:6).

*Do not neglect the spiritual gift within you, which was bestowed on you through
prophetic utterance with the laying on of hands by the presbytery* (1 Timothy 4:14).

One of the elementary teachings of Christ is impartation of spiritual gifts through the laying on of hands. This principle is found in the very roots of Jewish culture. In fact, it was the
reason why Jacob was blessed and Esau was cursed. The significance of the laying on of hands
is further demonstrated in the Book of Hebrews in that it is mentioned in the same context as
resurrection and eternal judgment.

Therefore leaving the elementary teaching about the Christ, let us press on to maturity, not laying again a foundation of repentance from dead works and of faith toward God, of instruction about washings and laying on of hands, and the resurrection of the dead and eternal judgment (Hebrews 6:1-2).

The Role of Grace

Through grace we receive the abilities of the Holy Spirit. These abilities equip us to work in the harvest. Grace is not just undeserved favor; it is also the operational power of God.

But to each one of us grace was given according to the measure of Christ's gift.... And He gave some as apostles, and some as prophets, and some as evangelists, and some as pastors and teachers, for the equipping of the saints for the work of service, to the building up of the body of Christ (Ephesians 4:7,11-12).

Determining the Strength of Your Gift

Although the gifts are imparted through the laying on of hands, you still must receive them from the one who imparts them to you by faith. Two things will determine the strength and "flavor" of your gifts:

1. The proportion of your faith determines how much grace you receive to operate in the gifts. In other words, the greater amount of faith you have inside you, the stronger the gifts will operate through you.

2. The type and level of grace that is resident in the one who is imparting the gift to you will determine what gift is given to you.

The following is an example of how grace and faith work: If we go to a soda fountain for a drink, the flavor of the drink is determined by the fountain—like *the grace* on a person's life who imparts the gift to us. The amount of the drink we are able to receive is determined by the size of the cup that we bring to the fountain—our faith.

It is important that we stay within the boundaries of our own faith and try not to copy another person's faith. We don't have to be profound to be powerful. Sometimes the simplest word touches people as deeply as something that seems heavy or profound.

You don't have to be profound to be powerful.

Since we have gifts that differ according to the grace given to us, each of us is to exercise them accordingly: if prophecy, according to the proportion of his faith (Romans 12:6).

The gifts of the Holy Spirit are not awards! We cannot earn them. Because the gifts are not a mark of maturity, we do not have to wait for our lives to be in perfect order to receive them. Nonetheless, we are instructed to *earnestly desire* which means, "to passionately pursue them."

How the Gifts Grow

Jesus expressed His opinion about growing your gifts through the parable of the talents—*if we **use** what we have received, more will be given to us. If we **do not use** what we have, even what we have will be taken away from us.* This principle applies to every aspect of the Kingdom of God. If we want to receive a deeper level of prophetic revelation, then we must be faithful with the level of insight that we have now. Some people who have only received one talent spend all of their time trying to figure out why someone else received more, instead of stewarding what they have been given to attain more!

For it is just like a man about to go on a journey, who called his own slaves and entrusted his possessions to them. To one he gave five talents, to another, two, and to another, one, each according to his own ability; and he went on his journey. Immediately the one who had received the five talents went and traded with them, and gained five more talents. In the same manner the one who had received the two talents gained two more.

But he who received the one talent went away, and dug a hole in the ground and hid his master's money. Now after a long time the master of those slaves came and settled accounts with them.

The one who had received the five talents came up and brought five more talents, saying, "Master, you entrusted five talents to me. See, I have gained five more talents." His master said to him, "Well done, good and faithful slave. You were faithful with a few things, I will put you in charge of many things; enter into the joy of your master."

Also the one who had received the two talents came up and said, "Master, you entrusted two talents to me. See, I have gained two more talents." His master said to him, "Well done, good and faithful slave. You were faithful with a few things, I will put you in charge of many things; enter into the joy of your master."

And the one also who had received the one talent came up and said, "Master, I knew you to be a hard man, reaping where you did not sow and gathering where you scattered no seed. And I was afraid, and went away and hid your talent in the ground. See, you have what is yours." But his master answered and said to him, "You wicked, lazy slave, you knew that I reap where I did not sow and gather where I scattered no seed. Then you ought to have put my money in the bank, and on my arrival I would have received my money back with interest. Therefore take away the talent from him, and give it to the one who has the ten talents" (Matthew 25:14-28).

In First Timothy, Paul exhorts Timothy to "be absorbed in" and practice his spiritual gift so that he would grow and set an example to others through his pursuit.

Do not neglect the spiritual gift within you, which was bestowed on you through prophetic utterance with the laying on of hands by the presbytery. Take pains with these things; be absorbed in them, so that your progress will be evident to all (1 Timothy 4:14-15).

In First Peter, we are exhorted to "employ" the gifts that have been given to us. If we don't become good stewards of the gifts that God has given us, He will give them to someone who will take responsibility for them. God has no unemployment insurance!

As each one has received a special gift, employ it in serving one another as good stewards of the manifold grace of God (1 Peter 4:10).

The Baptism of the Holy Spirit and Gifts

Jesus told His disciples to wait for the promise of the Father which, when received, would give them power from on high. The word *power*, in Greek, is the word *dunamis*, which is where we get the word *dynamite*. Therefore, the baptism in the Holy Spirit is the *power behind the gifts*. The gifts can be compared to the motor in a car, in the sense that the baptism in the Holy Spirit is the fuel!

...but you will receive power when the Holy Spirit has come upon you; and you shall be My witnesses both in Jerusalem, and in all Judea and Samaria, and even to the remotest part of the earth (Acts 1:8).

Questions to Ponder

1. What is the most common way to receive the gifts of the Spirit?

   _____

   _____

2. What role does grace have for those who receive impartation from someone else?

   _____

   _____

3. What part does faith play in receiving the gifts of the Holy Spirit?

   _____

   _____

4. How do we grow stronger in the gifts that we already have?

   _____

   _____

Questions for Group Discussion

1. First Corinthians 12:11 says that the Holy Spirit distributes His gifts as He wills. How does the Holy Spirit determine to whom He will give His gifts?

2. How many of the gifts of the Spirit can we actually have?

Life Application

Ask the Holy Spirit if you have been faithful with everything that He has given you. If you have not, ask Him for a plan for the areas where you have been afraid or apathetic. Remember that courage is fear that has said its prayers! It's been said that, "A coward dies a thousands deaths, but a brave person dies only once."

Chapter 7

Prophetic Etiquette

Most of us have experienced a right prophetic word in the wrong season or a wrong word in the right season! This chapter is all about **how to speak the right word in the right season**. Also discussed is what the proper delivery of a prophetic word should look like.

 Like apples of gold in settings of silver is a word spoken in right circumstances (Proverbs 25:11).

Many of us imagine something similar to the following example when we think of the prophetic ministry taking place in the church.

Many years ago when we first started attending a charismatic church, there was a woman who would abruptly stand up in the middle of the pastor's sermon. She would shake, tremble, and scream out a message in tongues nearly every Sunday. This was followed by an interpretation of equal volume, spoken in dramatic King James English.

Guidelines to Proper Prophetic Ministry

The following guidelines are not meant to be laws, but merely intended to give some "banks to the river." Without banks, the river becomes a flood. In a flood, the water typically does more damage than good.

Every culture has its own unique flavor and style. It is essential, however, to realize that it is not our culture or style that makes a word prophetic. What makes a word prophetic is God speaking through someone.

Therefore, my brethren, desire earnestly to prophesy, and do not forbid to speak in tongues. **But all things must be done properly and in an orderly manner** (1 Corinthians 14:39-40, emphasis added).

An important key to proper prophetic ministry: The spirit of the prophet is subject to the prophet. This means that the Holy Spirit normally subjects Himself to the vessel that He is using. People are not acting according to the standard set by Scripture when they say things like, "God made me do that" or "The Spirit came upon me and I had to jump up and speak that out."

The spirits of prophets are subject to prophets (1 Corinthians 14:32).

The following examples illustrate times when it is inappropriate to give a prophetic word:

1. When we are angry or have strong, negative emotional feelings toward the person or people for whom we have a prophetic word.

2. When we use prophecy as a "platform" to validate our personal doctrines or belief system. Example: "I, the Lord, say to you tonight thou shall not go to movies!"

3. When we have no relationship or accountability to the person or group of people receiving our prophecy. It is important for prophetic people to have a sense of ownership of the people to whom they are ministering. Too often people have an "us" and "them" attitude toward the people they are ministering to. This is unhealthy and dishonoring.

Authority = Accountability + Responsibility + Accessibility

Delivery of the Prophetic Word

The following are practical guidelines for ministering and delivering prophetic words:

1. It is not necessary or recommended to use King James English when prophesying. King James English will not validate that what we are saying is from God. It simply

means that we read the King James Version of the Bible. Incidentally, Jesus didn't speak King James English, nor did He sound like Shakespeare.

2. It is important that our demeanor matches that of the Holy Spirit's. In other words, it is just as important for us to correctly present the *tone* in which the Holy Spirit communicated the word to us as it is *what* He said. It is seldom necessary for us to yell—increasing the volume of our voice does not make the prophecy better. The *tone* of voice in which we say something to a person *communicates just as much as the words* themselves.

3. *Love* must be at the center of all that we do in Christ. When we are ministering in the gifts of the Spirit, our motive must always be to bring out the *best* in people.

What is the outcome then, brethren? When you assemble, each one has a psalm, has a teaching, has a revelation, has a tongue, has an interpretation. **Let all things be done for edification** (1 Corinthians 14:26, emphasis added).

4. In a church service, the appropriate way to deliver a prophetic word is to submit it to the person or persons in charge of the service. At our church, prophecies are submitted to "Gatekeepers" who are aware of what the Holy Spirit is doing with worship and what direction the sermon will take. These people are able to determine if a prophetic word will be fitting for a particular service. Remember, the goal of all prophecy is to present an accurate word in the right circumstances.

5. Phrases such as, "I the Lord say to you tonight," or "Thus saith the Lord," are seldom necessary. What makes a prophetic word the voice of God? *God* is the one who initiated it—not man. When the prophecy is judged, it will be evident whether it was the Lord speaking or not.

Negative and/or Judgmental Words

The Bible is clear that life and death are in our words. When we give people negative words, we often release death over them. Our goal is to be a part of a ministry that releases life and calls out the best in people.

Death and life are in the power of the tongue, and those who love it will eat its fruit (Proverbs 18:21).

Most of the time it is best to avoid giving negative or judgmental prophetic words.

Remember also that just because the word ends positively does not mean that it is an *encouraging* word. A good rule to follow: If you would not want to receive the word yourself, you should not give it to someone else.

> *A member of our prophetic team gave a pastor this word: "Like Job and his wife you are about to endure a season of great loss, but in the end, the Lord will restore you to double, just like He did for Job."*
>
> *Thankfully, this word was given to a mature pastor, otherwise the word could have been very damaging. The pastor did the right thing by bringing this word to our leadership and the team member was redirected in love.*

Warning or Judgment Words

The following guidelines will help if you receive multiple warning or judgment words.

1. Ask yourself if negative words are common to you. If a high percentage of the prophetic revelation you receive is negative, you may be the problem.

2. Occasionally the Lord will warn of upcoming dangerous or negative situations. He informs us so we might pray for our or someone else's safety. Pray until the burden lifts.

3. Ask the Holy Spirit for a prophetic word that releases life into the situation. Remember, prophetic ministry releases grace for things to change. Prophesying the answer will uplift our spirits and come against the darkness that is threatening us.

4. If the warning persists, we should submit the word to our leadership. Once it is given over to them and we have relinquished ownership, they are now responsible. God will speak to them as we pray for Him to give them wisdom and guidance regarding the word.

Accountability

At times we may feel that the Lord has spoken to us about our own lives. In other words, we have prophesied over *ourselves*. As with any other prophetic word, it should be judged. It is vitally important that we submit this word to those who have authority over us; just as we would if we had received it from someone else. This is especially true if the word involves direction.

When we articulate this type of word to leadership, we should not say, "*The Lord **told** me to do this.*" That opening statement dramatically reduces their ability to give us their input. After all, who wants to argue with God?

When people go to leadership for counsel, and begin a conversation with, "*The Lord **told** me to do this,*" in reality what they are often saying is, "*I don't want your opinion; I just want your blessing for what I want to do.*"

I was once speaking with a pastor who shared that he had divorced his wife because "God had told him to." He said that his son had a dream that he believed also validated his decision to leave his wife! While questioning him concerning his marriage, I asked him if his wife had committed adultery. "No," he replied, "nothing like that...she hated the ministry."

*I thought he was going to fall out of his chair when I told him that God did **not** tell him to leave his wife!*

Remember, we only have as much authority in God as we are willing to submit to.

If we only do what those in leadership over our lives tell us to do *when we agree with them*, that is *not* called submission, but rather "doing our own thing." We must invite leadership into our lives and learn to trust them more than we trust ourselves. Otherwise, if we ever become deceived in an area, the only way to find our way out of deception is to *trust someone else more than ourselves*. The very nature of deception is that *we do not know we are deceived!* If we *know* we are deceived, that is not called deception, but *stupidity*!

This doesn't mean that we should follow a leader whose life and ministry doesn't have good fruit. It also doesn't mean that we do something that the Bible clearly tells us is wrong just because a leader tells us to do it. We are to follow our leaders as they follow Christ!

BASIC TRAINING FOR THE PROPHETIC MINISTRY

Obey your leaders and submit to them, for they keep watch over your souls as those who will give an account. Let them do this with joy and not with grief, for this would be unprofitable for you (Hebrews 13:17).

Questions to Ponder

1. What are some reasons why it would be inappropriate to prophesy?

   _____

   _____

2. What are some things to watch for when delivering a prophetic word?

   _____

   _____

3. What is the proper procedure for delivering a prophetic word in a public service?

   _____

   _____

Questions for Group Discussion

1. Why do you think people sometimes yell or use King James English when delivering a prophetic word?

2. How do you determine the Holy Spirit's mood or attitude for the proper delivery of a prophetic word?

Life Application

Pray for the Holy Spirit to give you a prophetic word during a church service. Practice your prophetic protocol in delivering the word. Find the gatekeepers and give them the word that you believe the Lord gave you. Allow them to determine the authenticity and timing of the word. If you are given permission to deliver the word, be conscious of not just what to say but how to say it.

"It is you who are the sons of the prophets...."
(Acts 3:25)

"...he who believes in Me, the works that I do, he will do also; and greater works than these he will do; because I go to the Father"
(John 14:12)

Chapter 8

False Prophets

Much has been written about false prophets. This chapter discusses the facts and fallacies surrounding them, and explains why a false prophet is not someone who gives a bad prophetic word but rather is someone who has an evil heart.

What Makes a False Prophet?

There are two types of false prophets. The first type is comprised of people who have invited a spirit of divination into their lives. The gift, which enables them to prophesy, comes from an evil spirit and has nothing to do with God. The gift is from hell and these people have let their hearts turn to evil. What is important to note: although the word is coming from a spirit of divination, it can still be accurate! Acts chapter 16 illustrates this principle through a false prophetess who has the right word, but the wrong spirit.

It happened that as we were going to the place of prayer, a slave-girl having a spirit of divination met us, who was bringing her masters much profit by fortune-telling. Following after Paul and us, she kept crying out, saying, "These men are bond-servants of the Most High God, who are proclaiming to you the way of salvation." She continued doing this for many days. But Paul was greatly annoyed, and turned and said to the spirit, "I command you in the name of Jesus Christ to come out of her!" And it came out at that very moment (Acts 16:16-18).

The second type of false prophets is the group of people who receive a call on their lives to be a prophet or prophetess from birth or after they receive Christ, yet they later fall away from God. Interestingly, in Romans 11:29, it states that the gifts and callings of God are irrevocable. Even if we fall away from God, we would still be able to operate in the gifts. However, this gift would not be in our control, but would be turned over to the hands of the evil one. In Numbers chapters 22 through 24, we read about a false prophet named Balaam. It is clear in the Scripture that Balaam is getting his prophetic revelation from God, but he is trying to use his gift to curse God's people so he can make money. Balaam has a gift from God but a heart from hell.

False Prophets' Characteristics

According to Matthew, false prophets have certain characteristics.

Beware of the false prophets, who come to you in sheep's clothing, but inwardly are ravenous wolves. You will know them by their fruits. Grapes are not gathered from thorn bushes nor figs from thistles, are they? So every good tree bears good fruit, but the bad tree bears bad fruit. A good tree cannot produce bad fruit, nor can a bad tree produce good fruit. Every tree that does not bear good fruit is cut down and thrown into the fire. So then, you will know them by their fruits.

Not everyone who says to Me, "Lord, Lord," will enter the kingdom of heaven, but he who does the will of My Father who is in heaven will enter. Many will say to Me on that day, "Lord, Lord, did we not prophesy in Your name, and in Your name cast out demons, and in Your name perform many miracles?" And then I will declare to them, "I never knew you; depart from Me, you who practice lawlessness."

Therefore everyone who hears these words of Mine and acts on them, may be compared to a wise man who built his house on the rock. And the rain fell, and the floods came, and the winds blew and slammed against that house; and yet it did not fall, for it had been founded on the rock. Everyone who hears these words of Mine and does not act on them, will be like a foolish man who built his house on the sand. The rain fell, and the floods came, and the winds blew and slammed against that house; and it fell—and great was its fall (Matthew 7:15-27).

The following are the common threads that run through the lives of the type of false prophet described in Matthew chapter 7:

1. False prophets appear to be good—like sheep—but are really like wolves. They are the enemy of the sheep. The bad fruit that they bear is not a *false gift* but rather an *evil heart*. Remember, these people will say to Jesus, "Did we not prophesy in Your name and cast out demons in Your name?" But He will say to them, "*I never knew you.*" He calls them "*lawless.*" It is interesting how Jesus defines "lawless" in Matthew

chapter 7 in the description of the two different men building houses. He considered the one who *heard* His words but *did not act on them* to be lawless! Notice also that the Lord equates knowing Him with keeping His Word.

If you love Me, you will keep My commandments (John 14:15).

2. False prophets have their belief system founded on a *few pet* Scriptures (sand) and not the *whole* counsel of God (*the rock*). False prophets take certain Scriptures out of context that advocate their own agenda. They find Scriptures, pull them out of a story or an idea, and create a new meaning.

3. False prophets have power. Unfortunately, their goal is to use their power to lead people to themselves, instead of to Christ. A false prophet makes his or herself the answer instead of God! Some people have a desire to be needed so badly that they lead people to themselves through their ministries instead of leading them to God.

For false Christs and false prophets will arise and will show great signs and wonders, so as to mislead, if possible, even the elect (Matthew 24:24).

Discerning the Difference

According to John, there is a way to discern the difference between a true prophet and a false prophet. In the Book of First John, he gives us guidelines. The first verse of the text warns Christians to *not become false prophets by believing the wrong spirit*. This caution is sobering. Many Christians do not believe that evil spirits can influence them. One of the greatest deceptions in the church today is the idea that Christians cannot be deceived by the devil. The following Scripture passage clearly dispels that myth.

Beloved, do not believe every spirit, but test the spirits to see whether they are from God, because many false prophets have gone out into the world. By this you know the Spirit of God: every spirit that confesses that Jesus Christ has come in the flesh is from God; and every spirit that does not confess Jesus is not from God; this is the

spirit of the antichrist, of which you have heard that it is coming, and now it is already in the world (1 John 4:1-3).

Five Tests of a *True* Prophet

1. *Does the prophet believe in the redemptive work of the Son of God?*

One thing to note is that false prophets are *antichrist* in nature. They are *not* anti-*Jesus*. The word *Christ* means "the anointed one." The anointing is always related to the power of God. Beware of people who try to tell you that Jesus doesn't do miracles anymore. According to Paul in Second Corinthians chapter 11, there is *another* "Jesus" who is not the Christ (anointed one). The Jesus we serve was anointed yesterday, is anointed today, and will be anointed forever!

You are from God, little children, and have overcome them; because greater is He who is in you than he who is in the world. They are from the world; therefore they speak as from the world, and the world listens to them. We are from God; he who knows God listens to us; he who is not from God does not listen to us. By this we know the spirit of truth and the spirit of error (1 John 4:4-6).

2. *False prophets do not like to listen to anyone; in their own minds, **God** tells them everything.*

False prophets are hyper-spiritual in their conversations and begin most of their statements with, "The Lord said to me..." or "God told me...." I have found over the years that this is just a rather spiritual way of saying, "I don't want *your* input!" They are not under any authority but their own.

Beloved, let us love one another, for love is from God; and everyone who loves is born of God and knows God. The one who does not love does not know God, for God is love. By this the love of God was manifested in us, that God has sent His only begotten Son into the world so that we might live through Him. In this is love, not that we loved God, but that He loved us and sent His Son to be the propitiation for our sins. Beloved, if God so loved us, we also ought to love one another. No one has

seen God at any time; if we love one another, God abides in us, and His love is perfected in us.

By this we know that we abide in Him and He in us, because He has given us of His Spirit. We have seen and testify that the Father has sent the Son to be the Savior of the world. Whoever confesses that Jesus is the Son of God, God abides in him, and he in God. We have come to know and have believed the love which God has for us. God is love, and the one who abides in love abides in God, and God abides in him. By this, love is perfected with us, so that we may have confidence in the day of judgment; because as He is, so also are we in this world (1 John 4:7-17).

3. *False prophets are not motivated by love but are motivated by a need to be noticed.*

The central theme of all ministries must be the love of God. We must ask ourselves:

Am I in the ministry for the purpose of bringing out the best in people?

Do I have the kind of love that covers a multitude of sins?

We love, because He first loved us. If someone says, "I love God," and hates his brother, he is a liar; for the one who does not love his brother whom he has seen, cannot love God whom he has not seen. And this commandment we have from Him, that the one who loves God should love his brother also (1 John 4:19-21).

4. *False prophets commonly use fear to motivate people.*

"Doom and gloom" tend to be the main thrusts of the false prophets' message. They also say things like, "God showed me something about you, but I can't tell you." This kind of statement breeds insecurity in people. False prophets revel in thinking that they "have something on you" that you don't know about!

There is no fear in love; but perfect love casts out fear, because fear involves punishment, and the one who fears is not perfected in love (1 John 4:18).

5. *False prophets are not in covenant relationship with the Body of Christ.*

I have yet to observe a false prophet who has a healthy relationship with the local body they attend. Many do not even attend church at all. They wander from place to place looking for people who will listen to them. The word *covenant* means that we are not in a relationship for what we can get from people but rather for what we can give. Covenant relationships are costly. Jesus, in John 15:13, says, *"Greater love has no one than this, that one lay down his life for his friends."*

Leading People Out of Prophetic Deception

Confronting those who *believe* they are true prophets, but are not, can be a rather difficult situation. Most false prophets have been abused by authority much of their lives and therefore do not trust anyone. Fear is the number one reason why people become hyper-spiritual, and it results in religious deception. To make matters worse, many false prophets have a martyr's complex. The more they are confronted about their weirdness, the more validated they feel. They interpret attempts at correcting them as persecution that proves they are "standing for God" and against the unrighteous religious system! They say things like, "I don't believe in organized religion," when the real problem is that they don't like boundaries. Remember, Jesus calls them "lawless." Lawless people are those who want to live outside of authority.

So how can they be helped? First of all, the leaders of the flock must not be afraid to confront these people even though they may appear to know more than the leadership and may be intimidating. Remember, "All that wickedness needs to prosper is for righteous men to do nothing." It is also important to not react but instead respond to these people; otherwise, the cure can be worse than the disease. People like this are accustomed to criticism and rejection, and will use it to validate their "ministry."

They can, however, be won over by true, Godly discipline (not punishment). The difference between punishment and discipline: punishment says, "I will get even with you for the damage you have caused," but discipline says, "I love you too much to leave you broken."

The only hope for these people is when they begin to feel loved. As they experience the love of God, they can begin to trust the leadership to lead them out of their deception.

If they refuse to repent and submit to correction, they must be removed from fellowship; otherwise, they will lead others astray. As mentioned previously, the primary weakness of false prophets is that they draw people to themselves instead of to God. There is a very narrow window of time for leadership to deal with false prophets before they rally people to their defense *against* the leadership. They have an uncanny ability to attach themselves to the young or hurting sheep and are able to divide them from the flock. Finally, like wolves, they devour the sheep in deception.

Beware of false prophets!

Questions to Ponder

1. Name five things that distinguish a false prophet from a true prophet.

   _____

   _____

2. What is one of the main reasons why people become false prophets?

   _____

   _____

3. Why does opposing false prophets somehow seem to validate their ministry?

   _____

   _____

4. Is a person who gives inaccurate prophecies always a false prophet?

   _____

   _____

5. Can a person give accurate prophecies and still be a false prophet?

   _____

   _____

Questions for Group Discussion

1. In First John chapter 4, the beloved are warned not to become false prophets. How could someone who loves Jesus eventually fall into the category of a false prophet?

2. Do you see any of these tendencies in your own heart?

Life Application

Independence, fear, and pride all keep us from the deep relationships that we need with God and His people. It is so important that we have people in our lives in whom we trust more than we trust ourselves. Do you have a relationship with someone you would trust with your life? If that person told you that you have a problem, one that you don't see, would you believe that person even though it does not feel true? We need to build these kinds of relationships to keep us safe as we live on the edge. Go build a relationship with someone like that in authority.

Chapter 9

Practicing Prophecy

This chapter provides some practical lessons on various ways to practice the
Gift of Prophecy and Words of Knowledge. It is only in practicing that
your confidence grows and your accuracy increases.

Practicing the Gifts of the Spirit

Unfortunately, some Christians misunderstand the definition of practicing the gifts of the
Holy Spirit. We are not practicing so that the Holy Spirit can improve His gifts, but rather we
are practicing to *improve our ability to flow with what the Holy Spirit is doing*.

In the days of Samuel, Elijah, and Elisha, the *sons of the prophets* studied under the guidance
of these prophets in what was probably a school of the prophets. Although the sons of the
prophets were based out of Naioth in Ramah, they wandered throughout the wilderness practicing their prophecies while being mentored by these renowned prophets.

*Then Saul sent messengers to take David, but when they saw the company of the
prophets prophesying, with Samuel standing and presiding over them, the Spirit of
God came upon the messengers of Saul; and they also prophesied (1 Samuel 19:20).*

Practicing the gifts of the Spirit should take place in an atmosphere of love and a culture of
spiritual authority. Without being in submission to true spiritual authority, we are like a contractor who builds a skyscraper without a foundation. The first time the wind blows, it will fall
to the ground.

No Pain—No Gain

In the Book of First Timothy, Paul exhorts Timothy to minister in his spiritual gift beyond his comfort zone. Anyone who has ever performed physical exercise knows that there is little profit to exercising until your body feels a degree of pain. Therefore, if we wake up the morning after exercising and we're not sore, we would realize that the exercise only *maintained* our *current* condition!

> ## Reach beyond your comfort zone.

The same principle applies to our spiritual growth. If we only do what is *comfortable* for us, we will fail to grow. Whenever we are truly growing, there will always be an element of discomfort. You can look at it this way: The dogs of doom stand at the doors of destiny. In other words, the things you are afraid of often hold the greatest rewards.

Do not neglect the spiritual gift within you, which was bestowed on you through prophetic utterance with the laying on of hands by the presbytery. Take pains with these things; be absorbed in them, so that your progress will be evident to all (1 Timothy 4:14-15).

Put the Gift in the Fire

Paul, in Second Timothy 1:6, reminds Timothy to "*kindle afresh the gift of God.*" Looking to the Greek translation, this phrase signifies "putting the gift through the fire or joining the gift with fire." The next verse makes more sense now in this context; "*For God has not given us a spirit of fear, but of power and of love and of a sound mind*" (2 Tim. 1:7 NKJV).

Whenever we step out in faith, we must step over fear! Fear is the guard dog that is protecting the fortress of spiritual prosperity. When the dog starts barking, we can be sure that the treasure he is guarding is near. Most people do not allow their gifts to be forged in the fire of risk. The result: their gifts are weak and not tempered.

Therefore I remind you to stir up the gift of God which is in you through the laying on of my hands. For God has not given us a spirit of fear, but of power and of love and of a sound mind (2 Timothy 1:6-7 NKJV).

Suggestions for Practicing Prophecy

The following are practical suggestions for practicing the gifts of the Spirit.

1. *Prophesy your day.*

When you wake in the morning, pray and ask the Lord for information about something that will happen during your day. Write it down as clearly as you understand it. At the end of the day, check and see if the event that you prophesied to yourself happened. Also see how well you understood the specific details of the event(s).

2. *Practice words of knowledge.*

Go to a restaurant or public place of business and pray for the person who is providing a service for you. Ask the Lord for words of knowledge for the person. It is usually best if you do this when the person is not in your presence. Write down the words of knowledge on a piece of paper. Later you can "interview" the person concerning the words of knowledge you received.

For example, if you think the Lord showed you that the person you are receiving words for has three children; you can simply ask him or her if they have any children. If the answer is yes, you can inquire how many, etc. When you are first learning, I would suggest you not tell the person that you have words of knowledge from God. In the beginning, this practice is more about you growing in your gift than about ministering. As your ability to hear the voice of the Holy Spirit improves, you will begin to step out in boldness and faith.

3. *Team up with another person.*

Enlist the help of a prayer partner. Pray for one another and ask the Lord for words of knowledge for each other. Take turns sharing what you believe God has shown you. Let the recipient judge the word you are giving to them. Obviously, this works best if both of you are trying to grow in your spiritual gifts. It is important in this exercise to be extremely truthful with one another so as to gain an honest assessment of how you are doing.

4. *Words of knowledge for healing.*

You can practice words of knowledge for healing in a group setting by simply praying and asking the Lord to show you anyone who is experiencing illness or pain. This will often come as a sensation in your body that directly coincides with the part of someone else's body that the

Lord wants to heal. If it is appropriate in the meeting, ask the group if anyone has the specific problem in their body. Then afterward, you should pray for that person and experience the joy of seeing the Lord heal them!

5. *Prophesying as a group.*

Another way to practice in a group setting is to chose one member of the group and have the others prophesy to that person. As the words are given, ask a member of the group to write them down. After an adequate number of prophetic words are given, ask the person who received the prophetic words to judge the words and give feedback to the group about the accuracy of the word.

6. *Prophetic intercession.*

Prophetic intercession is practiced as we pray. Often in prayer the Lord will give you insight into people's lives. Prophesy the answer to each of these issues that you see in the lives of these people and then ask the Lord to let your paths cross that day. You will be amazed at how many times the Lord will bring people to your mind to pray for—people you haven't seen in months, or even years. Most likely, you will soon hear from them.

Questions to Ponder

1. Name the greatest obstacle that we must overcome to see our gifts grow.

_____

_____

2. How can we tell when we are growing in our gifts?

_____

_____

3. Name three ways in which we can practice our spiritual gifts.

_____

_____

Questions for Group Discussion

1. Share one experience that you had when you stepped over fear into faith. What did you learn from the experience?

2. What is your greatest fear when you consider walking in the fullness of your gifts?

3. What are you going to do about your fear?

Life Application

Create a plan to overcome your greatest fears. Then become accountable to someone to carry out your plan.

"It is you who are the sons of the prophets...."
(Acts 3:25)

"...he who believes in Me, the works that I do, he will do also; and greater works than these he will do; because I go to the Father"
(John 14:12)

Epilogue

Each and every day the world wakes up to the bad news of a planet in decay. Depression and death press into our minds and steal our courage. Even our homes that were once safe places for children to grow up in love have become, for many, battlefields where little ones must run for cover. Sticks and stones are breaking their bones and names are taking away their future.

Yet in all of this confusion, there is still a God who only rested one day. His creative proclamations that instilled life and goodness in the Book of Genesis perpetuate through His vessels even to this day. It is He who reigns supremely over all of His creation. He is not depressed, confused, afraid, or perplexed over the darkness of this planet. He speaks into those who are formless and void, and life is the result of His words!

I know a man who 25 years ago had a nervous breakdown. The breakdown lasted for more than three and a half years. His hands trembled so violently that he could not even bring a glass of water to his lips without using both hands. He would sweat so profusely at night from fear and anxiety that his wife would have to get up in the middle of the night and change the soaking wet sheets. As time went on he began to lose his mind and many times a day he would envision himself murdering people—or worse. Demons visited and tormented him throughout the night.

Then one afternoon some friends persuaded him to attend a Christian retreat in the mountains. That day a prophet was speaking at the meeting. He called the young man out of the crowd and prophesied to him. He said, "*The Lord has called you to be a pillar in the house of God. You shall be a teacher and a pastor to His people. Strength is in you!*"

The war in that man's life was won that day. I know that man very well—*I am that man!*

Never underestimate the redemptive power of God's prophetic ministry. There are many people starving to know who they *really* are. *You* have the ability to alter the history of people who are lost and broken.

Don't disappoint them.

"It is you who are the sons of the prophets...." (Acts 3:25)

"...he who believes in Me, the works that I do, he will do also; and greater works than these he will do; because I go to the Father" (John 14:12)

BASIC TRAINING BASIC

BASIC

Appendix

The forms on the following pages were created to help you keep track of your dreams, visions, and prophecies. Recording your experiences will assist you in developing accountability that builds up your faith. These records may be used as learning and/or teaching tools similar to the films that athletes use of their previous games to improve their abilities. You may want to copy the pages and create a prophetic journal.

Let the journey begin!

"It is you who are the sons of the prophets...."
(Acts 3:25)

"...he who believes in Me, the works that I do, he will do also; and greater works than these he will do; because I go to the Father"
(John 14:12)

Dreams & Visions

Date: _____

Dream or Vision Description:

_____
_____
_____
_____

Interpretation:

_____
_____
_____
_____

Application:

_____
_____
_____
_____

Date of fulfillment: _____

Dreams & Visions

Date: _____

Dream or Vision Description:

_____
_____
_____
_____

Interpretation:

_____
_____
_____
_____

Application:

_____
_____
_____
_____

Date of fulfillment: _____

Dreams & Visions

Date: _____

Dream or Vision Description:

_____

_____

_____

_____

Interpretation:

_____

_____

_____

_____

Application:

_____

_____

_____

_____

Date of fulfillment: _____

Dreams & Visions

Date: _____

Dream or Vision Description:

_____

_____

_____

_____

Interpretation:

_____

_____

_____

_____

Application:

_____

_____

_____

_____

Date of fulfillment: _____

Dreams & Visions

Date: _____

Dream or Vision Description:

_____

_____

_____

_____

Interpretation:

_____

_____

_____

_____

Application:

_____

_____

_____

_____

Date of fulfillment: _____

Dreams & Visions

Date: _____

Dream or Vision Description:

_____
_____
_____
_____

Interpretation:

_____
_____
_____
_____

Application:

_____
_____
_____
_____

Date of fulfillment: _____

Dreams & Visions

Date: _____

Dream or Vision Description:

_____

_____

_____

_____

Interpretation:

_____

_____

_____

_____

Application:

_____

_____

_____

_____

Date of fulfillment: _____

Dreams & Visions

Date: _____

Dream or Vision Description:

_____

_____

_____

_____

Interpretation:

_____

_____

_____

_____

Application:

_____

_____

_____

_____

Date of fulfillment: _____

Prophetic Words

Date: _____

_____

_____

_____

_____

_____

Word given by: _____ Word given to: _____

Date: _____

_____

_____

_____

_____

_____

Word given by: _____ Word given to: _____

Date: _____

_____

_____

_____

_____

_____

Word given by: _____ Word given to: _____

Prophetic Words

Date: _____

_____

_____

_____

_____

_____

Word given by: _____ Word given to: _____

Date: _____

_____

_____

_____

_____

_____

Word given by: _____ Word given to: _____

Date: _____

_____

_____

_____

_____

_____

Word given by: _____ Word given to: _____

Prophetic Words

Date: _____

_____

_____

_____

_____

_____

Word given by: _____ Word given to: _____

Date: _____

_____

_____

_____

_____

_____

Word given by: _____ Word given to: _____

Date: _____

_____

_____

_____

_____

_____

Word given by: _____ Word given to: _____

Prophetic Words

Date: _____

_____

_____

_____

_____

_____

Word given by: _____ Word given to: _____

Date: _____

_____

_____

_____

_____

_____

Word given by: _____ Word given to: _____

Date: _____

_____

_____

_____

_____

_____

Word given by: _____ Word given to: _____

For The Love of God (CD)

This is a journey into the heart of God viewed through the eyes of a boy and his grandfather. You'll laugh and cry yourself into a new place of love, and find a fresh place of passion as you discover the One who has been waiting for all eternity just to dance this last dance with you. This message will surprise you.

From Paupers to Princes (CD)

This powerful message is taken from Kris' personal journey out of a life of insignificance, into a place of leadership. His words will confront the "pauper" and call out the "prince" in you. Kris explores the destructive nature of the "pauper" mentality and brings wisdom to escape its claws.

Purity (CD)

Kris explores the battle over virginity and equips you with some powerful weapons to win. This message also provides hope for those who have lost this battle and leads them back to victory

What is That...On Your Lens? (CD)

All of us question what we see at times, but we seldom question how we see. If we have a booger on the lens of our life, it may appear that the world is full of people with boogers on them—when in fact, we are living in a virtual reality. In this humorous message you will laugh your way into truth as Kris lays a foundation of freedom that will alter the course of your history. This message is guaranteed to change the way you see the world!

Holy Affection (CD)

Many have withdrawn their affection because they fear what people may think. Affection is the vehicle in which God intended love to flow. Without it, we have created an atmosphere of sterile Christianity. Kris' message puts holy affection back into the place where God intended it to be—pure, holy, and undefiled.

Back to the Future (CD)

A powerful exhortation about how to let go of your past and make sure it doesn't infect your future.

Going Down to the Top (CD)

A revelatory message about the true power of humility and servanthood unlike you've heard before. In this revelatory teaching, the secrets that cause Holy Spirit activity to be released in the local church are explored. This teaching is a must for everyone in leadership, and could very possibly change you forever.

Life is Messy (CD)

Kris shares about the benefits of taking risks, even when they make your life messy!

The New Wineskin (CD)

In this revelatory teaching, the secrets that cause Holy Spirit activity to be released in the local church are explored. This teaching is a must for everyone in leadership.

Rebuilding the Altar (CD)

Kris brings to light the inheritance we receive when all generations—young and old—join hearts. This teaching will bring power into your daily walk with God.

Fear Is Not Your Friend! (CD)

Tape 1 - Fear is a spirit and it doesn't belong to you. If you are to walk in the power of the Spirit, you must realize that fear is a lie the enemy uses to stop you from being victorious. Tape 2 - The fear of rejection by people will stop you from walking as God would have you walk. Learn to walk in faith, not in fear.

Here Come the Prophets (CD)

Tape 1- Kris Vallotton's testimony about a prophet raised up in Northern California. This is an alarming account of personal deliverance, illustrating how God groomed Kris for this hour. Tape 2 - In this message, Pastor Bill Johnson brings the much needed honor to the prophet, while maintaining the individual's responsibility to hear from God for themselves. Prophets are God's idea, fashioned just for us. Learning how to receive this gift into our lives pays great dividends as we press on to know the Lord, and make Him known.

Leadership for a New Millennium (CD

This powerful leadership message is an adventure into the "new wineskin" of God's order. This series was taken from the conference theme: Establishing Church Government. These truths about spiritual oversight are both prophetic in their foresight and practical in their insight. This message will have a significant impact on anyone who is in any form of leadership in the Body of Christ.

Ravaging the Gates of Hell: A Personal Journey (CD)

A humorous but sobering look into the reasons why evil spirits continue to influence Christians today. Discover how we give the devil permission to use our authority against us and learn what to do about it. This series is a must for people who struggle with sin habits, emotional problems, or demonic visitations.

Seasons of Your Life (CD)

Kris explores the spiritual seasons of our life. Whether you're in a time of fruitlessness or burnout in your walk with God, this is a perfect message for you.

The Conquest of Your Promised Land: A Prophetic Journey (CD)

In this series, Kris takes you on a journey through the Book of Joshua where you will discover the secrets of one of the greatest leaders in all of history. Walk with Joshua from the death of Moses to the conquest of the Promised Land and partake of his victory in your own life. Be ready for a change!

Ministering in the Spirit of Elijah (CD)

In this series, Kris is teaching practical lessons that are intended to release God's people into new levels of the prophetic ministry. You will learn the language of Heaven that destroys the works of hell. It is our prayer that you will experience the Holy Spirit's power as you listen to His voice.

To order these products and more, please visit our website at:
www.kvministries.com